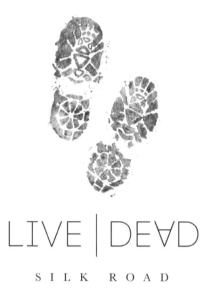

LIVE | DEAD

S I L K   R O A D

LIVE DEAD TOGETHER

a Practice in Group Abiding

BY BOOTS ON THE GROUND
MISSIONARIES ALONG THE SILK ROAD

Published by Live Dead Publishing
1445 N. Boonville Ave, Springfield, Missouri 65802

Published in partnership with The Stone Table (TheStoneTable.org)

Cover design, typesetting, and interior design by Prodigy Pixel
(www.prodigypixel.com).

ISBN-13: 978-0-9981789-6-7

Printed in the United States of America

— TABLE OF CONTENTS —

PREFACE

"IF YOU REMAIN IN ME
AND I IN YOU,

you will bear much fruit;

APART FROM ME

you can do nothing."

~ *Jesus* ~

(JOHN 15:5)

I grew up in a typical, late-20th-century evangelical environment in North America: a lot of Christian activities, Sunday church services with a primary speaker and a listening congregation, and personal quiet time. In late elementary school, I received a Bible with a checklist in it so I could track my progress as I read through the Bible. Sunday school teachers and youth group leaders were keen on teaching me and my classmates how to have good "devotions" with the Lord. I'm so incredibly grateful for those men and women who lovingly invested in me as a young man.

Jesus' invitation to abide in Him is often worked out these days in personal devotional practices but following Jesus in close companionship with other believers has been the norm for most of the history of the Christian faith. The New Testament is littered with dozens of "one another" statements, and most of the fruit of the Spirit found in Galatians 5 are impossible to bear without others around. While I was taught a lot about how to establish a "personal devotional life," I was not taught much about "abiding together" with the body of Christ. We went to church, but a common question I encountered in high school and university was, "Why do we need to go to church? Why do we need the body of Christ? As long as I'm hanging out with Jesus in my devotions, am I not okay?" I'm thankful that through those years I never fell out of the habit of gathering with others.

Live Dead emphasizes abiding with Jesus, and even abiding in extravagant and lavish ways. We talk about time spent in the presence of Jesus as being simultaneously our first priority and our chief methodology. We prioritize Jesus because of who He is: He is worthy of ranking number one in our day. We also recognize that Jesus promises it is only through a life-giving connection to

Him that we bear fruit in our lives. *The Live Dead Journal* (and its successors *Live Dead The Journey*, *Live Dead The Story*, *Live Dead Joy*, etc.) has served as a foundational tool for developing various way of entering and lingering in the presence of the Lord, but aside from an encouragement in the introductory material, little is said about abiding in a group. Abiding has always been about drawing near to Jesus both alone and in community. The original *Journal* was focused toward revitalizing and engaging the personal devotional life of Jesus' followers. *Live Dead Together* was especially born to reinvigorate and shape our practices of gathering together to meet with God and one another.

My hope is that as you work through this book, you will meet with the Lord as you gather together in your community. May the Lord speak to you, challenge you, encourage you, and build you up through one another as all of you, together, strive to grow in your knowledge of Him, relationship with Him, and reflection of His ways in our world.

D. JUMP

INTRODUCTION

Years ago, as my husband and I left a missionary training seminar, Dick Brogden casually handed me *The Live Dead Journal*. Strolling along with the crowd, he suggested that perhaps someday the region we worked with would be a part of the Live Dead movement. Not giving it much thought, I predictably put the *Journal* on a shelf to collect dust. Devotional books can be so anemic compared to the meatiness of Scripture itself, but months later I discovered this was not the case with *The Live Dead Journal*. In fact, I found it to be one of the most relevant devotionals to my life as a missionary among an unreached people group I ever read. Its value-based focus on character-depth and raw, unmanufactured stories of life as a missionary resonated with me.

Inevitably, Dick's prophetic suggestion came to pass and Live Dead Silk Road came into being. With a good deal of intentionality, creativity, and godly stubbornness, a training center known as the Launch Team was formed, and those of us who were on the field before the genesis of Live Dead Silk Road received the invitation to be grandfathered in as Live Dead Silk Road's alpha-test church planting teams. My heart to see the church planted in places with the least access to the gospel in addition to my personal calling to the region we colloquially call the "Silk Road" is what made joining the Live Dead community make sense. My heart for this work also provided the impetus for this book—the tenth book in the Live Dead series. Now perhaps you will be part of Live Dead someday. In fact, by reading, abiding together, and praying with us, you already are.

Purpose

As a guide in cultivating group abiding, this book is about waiting in God's presence together as a body of believers, reading, reflecting, discussing, learning, and, most of all, actively responding to His Word. It is not a curriculum and it is certainly not the authority on church devotional practices. Rather, this book is meant to serve as a tool designed to grow in each of us the vibrant, Christ-like character and tangible spiritual practices necessary to reach the hundreds of unreached people groups along the Silk Road who currently have no access to the good news of Jesus. The approach and purpose here is multi-faceted:

Cultivate Corporate Abiding

The Live Dead community encourages giving a tenth of your time—approximately 2.5 hours each day to engage in devotional practices for the purpose of abiding in Jesus (John 15). While this obviously includes intentionally set-aside times dedicated to personal Bible reading and prayer, this book expands the concept of abiding to include group settings as well. Our challenge is to be better as a body of believers at lingering in God's presence and hearing from Him in a way that guides our corporate vision. Some of the most fundamental elements of corporate worship have been included as well as an intentional selection of Scripture passages. However, please take the provided format as a guideline, not a rule. Corporate abiding is not about checking a spiritual task off a list or finishing every discussion question, but about soaking up the Word and discerning how we as a community of Jesus-followers can respond in humble obedience to what God is teaching us.

Embrace Values

The Live Dead community is guided by twelve values that are paramount to the work of seeing the church planted among the unreached. This book purposes to reinforce those values through short, true narratives demonstrating how those values are being embraced by boots-on-the-ground workers as they encounter people along the Silk Road. We hope that you engage with these values as you read and intercede, praying also that God will build in you what is necessary to do your part in taking His good news to the unreached.

Introduce Key Strategies

Each Live Dead area has their own unique flavors and challenges. This book purposes to provide a framework for strategic commitments that are particularly emphasized and implemented in Live Dead Silk Road. While character will always be of vital importance, the development of ministry competence through resourcing, training, and practice gives additional traction to the task of church planting. We hope that these practical strategies will prepare your hearts and minds as you pray about whether God is leading you to come be part of a church planting team on the Silk Road.

Inspire Prayer for Unreached People Groups (UPGs)

While the term may sound technical and even sterile,

[1] Names have been changed to protect the identities of those who have been written about; otherwise, the stories are faithful to what was experienced.

[2] Most statistics presented were gleaned from Joshua Project (http://joshuaproject.net).

unreached people groups represent real people—friends, neighbors, community acquaintances, and countless more that our boots-on-the-ground missionaries encounter on a daily basis. Why are such great swaths of ethno-linguistic groups untouched with the story of Jesus? Many are in hostile environments, some simply too remote for people to get to, and most steeped in religious ideologies that make no concessions for questioning, dialogue, and discovery. These people will not be reached with simple solutions, safe ventures, or sheer manpower. The church must be willing to sacrifice, perhaps even lay down lives. The church must be willing to plead for God's intervention. Through short, true narratives[1] and specific prayer requests, this book aims to help you feel a personal connection with the people who live along the Silk Road and to challenge your commitment to pray for them.

As a note, although there are hundreds of UPGs along the Silk Road, this book is limited to highlighting only twenty-four in the number of chapters included. Through a collaborative, prayerful effort we have chosen to introduce those people groups that someone living in the Silk Road region would be most likely encounter.[2]

Intended Audience

This book is intended for a small group of Jesus-followers who commit to meet regularly and abide together. Although not limited to, we wrote with campus ministries in mind in a two-part format that can be conveniently utilized over the course of two school semesters. If a small group meets once a week, each part would take twelve weeks. This gives space for settling into a new semester and any holidays that might interfere with a small group meeting over the course of a typical 15-week semester. This format would also easily fit well for a church small group or Sunday school class.

For the sake of flow and orderliness there are time guidelines for each practice (totaling about ninety minutes), but you should be more concerned about following the Holy Spirit's leading than filling a time slot. This is a resource for you and your community. Keeping the purpose of the book as outlined above in mind, feel free to adapt and tweak it to whatever format and time frame is most suitable for your group. Most groups, particularly those with time constraints, may not be able to go through every journaling question. That is okay; the questions can be used for further individual reflection and response once the time set aside for corporate abiding is done. Even processing through it on a daily basis or as an individual exercise in abiding will be fruitful, as long as space is created for engaging with Jesus and allowing God to prune and water as He sees fit. A weekly abiding supplement for individual use is included at the end of the book to go hand in hand with the group abiding times.

Acknowledgments

I want to express gratitude to my colleagues, the dear Silk Road boots-on-the-ground missionaries, who have squeezed their hearts into a few descriptive paragraphs so that more will intercede for and begin to love the unreached peoples for whom they have already been laboring. Thanks to everyone who was part of this collaborative effort and for giving me the opportunity to formulate and edit its content. My prayer is that it will be a great help to everyone who walks through its pages.

R. M., EDITOR

YOU ARE THE

salt of the earth;

YOU ARE THE

light of the world;

as you go, glorify God.

THE DEVOTIONAL PRACTICE

INVITING IN

Inviting In *is the opening bookend to our time of abiding, a time to quiet our spirits and ask God's Holy Spirit to mentor and guide us as we walk forward. Together recite the suggested short Biblical prayer and then spend one or two minutes in silence. Try to shelf your mental clutter and focus on being available to hear from the Lord.*

INWARD PRAYER (10 minutes)

Inward Prayer *is a time to survey our hearts, assess our actions, and take care of sin issues. Individually read the suggested verse of confession as an honest, personal prayer. Take a moment to examine yourself. Quietly pray for forgiveness where necessary. Even if not a sin issue, talk to the Lord about areas in which you need help. If the Holy Spirit is prompting you to confess a sin to the group or ask forgiveness from a specific person, this is the time to do that. Embrace repentance. This is also an appropriate time to seek accountability. If you did not obey last week's promptings, admit it to a friend or the group and make a plan for how you will obey this week.*

WORSHIP (15 minutes)

Worship *is a time to thank and honor God. Sing two or three hymns or indigenously appropriate worship songs. This is also a wonderful juncture to take communion together.*

WORD (10 minutes)

Word *time is for reading the selected Scripture passage together out loud. Reading the passage individually at least once before meeting together is recommended.*

RESPONSE (25 minutes)

Response *is a time to engage with the portion of Scripture read. As a group explore the message God is communicating through the text and then create a plan of active obedience to Him in response. Questions are provided to help prompt discussion and discovery.*

OUTWARD PRAYER (30 minutes)

Outward Prayer *is a time to pray for each other as well as for interceding for the unreached world. Take a few minutes to pray together for the wisdom and strength to deliberately follow-through on your plans of action. Take the next few minutes to intercede for the unsaved people in your life. Ask the Lord to help you see and love the peoples who need to meet Him. Please continue to use the majority of this time to intercede for the highlighted Silk Road unreached people groups.*

SENDING OUT

Sending Out *is the closing bookend to our time of abiding. It is a commissioning. After this sacred time with the Lord and the body of believers, you each now have the opportunity to take what has been deposited in you and invest it in the family, friends, neighbors, co-workers, fellow students, and "chance encounters" that God puts in your life. Have the host of this abiding time read the suggested benediction and then proceed to go, grow, obey, share, and make Jesus famous.*

PROLOGUE

Weathered hands place a copious plate of fresh fruit on the table, a pleasant afterthought to the summer evening's meal. A plastic table cloth flitters at the edges. Aunt Aisha fiddles with her headscarf. Her eyes crease with a smile—an invitation to partake of the good fruit.

The grapes in particular are as sweet as the memory we make as we eat them together with our new friends. Juicy, nourishing. Earlier that day we waded through the vineyard, letting our fingers sweep over the product of hard work, sweat, and sunburn. Harvest has its cost, the least of which are wrinkle lines.

The vines are twisted and knotted, complicated, intricate, beautiful, strong, and life-giving. The branches firmly planted in the vine bear good fruit. The branches that do not, disintegrate; their fruit falling to the ground rotting in a disgusting fermented stench. This is the law of nature, but also an echo of a spiritual promise.

Jesus taught that He is the vine and we are the branches. Are we laboring in love to remain connected to Him—to abide in Him? Are our lives bearing good fruit?

For Aunt Aisha's sake, I hope so. Until our "chance encounter" and a kind invitation to her village, she had not once heard that, in great love, Jesus came to offer His life as a sacrificial payment for the sin that separates her from God—the sin, the shame, the separation of which she is keenly aware and the good news of saving grace of which she is not.

So it is with the majority of people across the Silk Road, the intricate expanse of coastal shorelines, high plains, and mountain peaks throughout the Central Eurasian region. Each Aisha, every Ahmet in dire need of consistent prayer, the persistent presence of Christ-followers, and the relentless proclamation of salvation through *Isa Mesih*, Jesus Christ.

LIVE | DEAD

SILK ROAD

PART ONE

Learning How To Follow Jesus

through responses to the gospel narrative
with emphasis on Live Dead values

INVITING IN (recite together)

Lord, you are our refuge,
our strength, and our help.

TEACH US TO STOP STRIVING,

To be still & know
That you are God.

You will be exalted
AMONG THE NATIONS;
You will be exalted
IN THE EARTH.

(BASED ON PSALMS 46:1, 10)

INWARD PRAYER (10 minutes)

Read individually

> Search me, God, and know my heart; test me and know my anxious thoughts. See if there is any offensive way in me, and lead me in the way everlasting. (Psalms 139:23, 24).

Silence

Confession & Accountability

How am I? What struggles am I facing today?

What is God's truth in the midst of this struggle?

Is there anything in my life that is creating a barrier between me and God or between me and a person in my life? If so, what should I do about it?

Reflect on God's forgiveness. Thank God for the help He is ready to give.

WORSHIP (15 minutes)

Sing together

Communion

WORD (10 minutes)

Read out loud together

      BIBLE STORY: The fall of Adam and Eve (Gen. 2:4–3:24)

      BIBLE TEACHING: Sin and shame separate us from God (Rom. 3:9–24)

RESPONSE (25 minutes)

Respond to the Word as a group or in pairs

What is God depositing IN your heart and mind through these Scriptures?

- *How would you summarize these passages?*

- *What is the key verse?*

- *What is the Lord teaching you through these passages?*

How can you conform to the image of Christ by living this OUT?

- *What attitude or way of thinking do I need to change?*

- *What action do I need to take?*

- *How will I do this? When will I do this?*

- *Who will keep me accountable?*

As you live this out, how will you express Jesus to those AROUND you?

- *How can I use these passages to tell someone about Jesus?*

- *Who will I share this with this week?*

- *As practice, rewrite or re-tell your summary of these passages and explain how they help you know Jesus.*

OUTWARD PRAYER (30 minutes)

Pray for each other

Pray for the people with whom you'll share

Pray for the Silk Road UPG on the following page

UNREACHED PEOPLE GROUP: *Tajik*

Shukrona is the strictest Muslim woman I have met since moving to Tajikistan.

One day Shukrona came over wearing a very conservative version of our local dress, a *korta*, a vibrantly floral dress with matching pants underneath that covers nearly every inch of her body even in the heat of the summer. She never removed her head covering, even in my home without a man present. (This, by the way, is a favorite thing for me—when my friends walk in, sit down at my table, and take off their head covering. It means we're all about to be real with each other.) We sat together at my kitchen table and she shared the challenges in her life—feeling like her boss, her family, and even her own mother underestimated her potential, feeling like she had no place of value either in the home or workplace. We soon found ourselves praying together, and I directed our prayers to Jesus. As we prayed, I found her overcome with emotion. It was evident the Holy Spirit was working. Everything about my friend looked "closed," but her heart was wide open to Him.

The kindness and palpable love of Jesus is oftentimes overwhelming for my Muslim friends. Many are abused by their husbands and in-laws in every possible way. As it was for this friend, she was overwhelmed. But I quickly discovered her loyalty to her religion as it had her on her feet minutes later searching for a towel to use as a makeshift prayer mat so she could pray to her Allah. I stood, shocked. The stronghold of Islam had her praying her Arabic prayers only minutes after seeing a glimpse of Jesus. My friends are open, but the stronghold is real.

One of my friends, a local Tajik believer, once told me that family members argued about the Holy Bible. One was reading it and another condemned it by saying, "Don't read that book. I hear it steals your soul." I laughed—because it's true! The Word of God is living and active, and we believe here in Tajikistan His Word and His palpable love will steal souls out of Islam.

Abiding

Intimacy with Jesus will define us and guide us in all we do. Each day's best is realized when it includes extravagant time in His presence. Abiding in Him personally and corporately empowers us to bear much fruit.

PRAY that missionaries will be uncompromising in their commitment to abiding in Jesus through a daily, dedicated time of centering on God's Word and prayer as well as through the ongoing practice of His presence.

PRAY that as Tajik believers devote themselves to abide in Jesus, they will find the strength and courage to remain in their home villages, despite persecution against them, for the sake of reaching their communities with the good news.

PRAY for the over 7,000,000 Tajik in Tajikistan, as well as millions more Tajik living in neighboring countries and throughout the globe, whose souls are left in darkness without Jesus.

SENDING OUT (read by host)

YOU ARE THE

salt of the Earth

YOU ARE THE

light of the world.

As you go, glorify God.

(BASED ON MATTHEW 5:13-14)

INVITING IN (recite together)

*Lord, you are our refuge,
our strength, and our help.*

TEACH US TO STOP STRIVING,

To be still & know
That you are God.

You will be exalted
AMONG THE NATIONS;
You will be exalted
IN THE EARTH.

(BASED ON PSALMS 46:1, 10)

INWARD PRAYER (10 minutes)

Read individually

> Search me, God, and know my heart; test me and know my anxious thoughts. See if there is any offensive way in me, and lead me in the way everlasting. (Psalms 139:23, 24).

Silence

Confession & Accountability

How am I? What struggles am I facing today?

What is God's truth in the midst of this struggle?

Is there anything in my life that is creating a barrier between me and God or between me and a person in my life? If so, what should I do about it?

Reflect on God's forgiveness. Thank God for the help He is ready to give.

WORSHIP (15 minutes)

Sing together

Communion

WORD (10 minutes)

Read out loud together

>   **BIBLE STORY:** A substitute for Abraham's son (Gen. 22:1–18)

>   **BIBLE TEACHING:** Jesus sacrificially died in our place (Heb. 9:19–10:10)

RESPONSE (25 minutes)

Respond to the Word as a group or in pairs

What is God depositing IN your heart and mind through these Scriptures?

>   • *How would you summarize these passages?*

>   • *What is the key verse?*

- *What is the Lord teaching you through these passages?*

How can you conform to the image of Christ by living this OUT?

- *What attitude or way of thinking do I need to change?*

- *What action do I need to take?*

- *How will I do this? When will I do this?*

- *Who will keep me accountable?*

As you live this out, how will you express Jesus to those AROUND you?

- *How can I use these passages to tell someone about Jesus?*

- *Who will I share this with this week?*

- *As practice, rewrite or re-tell your summary of these passages and explain how they help you know Jesus.*

OUTWARD PRAYER (30 minutes)

Pray for each other

Pray for the people with whom you'll share

Pray for the Silk Road UPG on the following page

UNREACHED PEOPLE GROUP: Uyghur

Back home in the rural hills overlooking China's western border, the men of the village spent their free time resting their weary knees while drinking milky-brown tea and mulling over the same weathered topics they always talked about. Abu Bakhr had been warned more than once of the evils of the West and the polytheistic, pig-eating, drunkard Christians. Of course, none of them had ever met a Christian and did not expect Abu Bakhr to meet one either when he went to this nearby Turkic-speaking, Muslim country as a student.

Dilara's round face, framed by her soft blue hijab, beamed as I handed her the Bible she asked me for. Abu Bakhr peered at it skeptically. Just the day before, he insisted foreigners passed out Bibles with $100 bills, bribing people, as if any Uyghur would be weak enough to accept the perverted Christian religion. Still, he was curious, too.

I knew realistically that when Dilara and Abu Bakhr returned from their studies abroad, home to East Turkistan, that Dilara would not have the freedom to explore this book. As in most patriarchal societies along the Silk Road, as a young man, Abu Bakhr might have a slight measure more independence, but fear of societal pressure runs strong in all human veins.

Character

Who we are will drive what we do. Integrity, humility, and authenticity are just as important as competence.

PRAY that missionaries' commitment to integrity will break down misconceptions about Christian life and faith.

PRAY that Muslim background believers (MBBs) along the Silk Road would understand the strategic possibility of reaching out to near-linguistic neighbors and be emboldened by the love of Christ to do so.

PRAY that the 360,400 Uyghurs scattered across the Silk Road and millions more in western China would gain unhindered access to the Word of God and the untainted message of Jesus.

SENDING OUT (read by host)

YOU ARE THE

salt of the Earth

YOU ARE THE

light of the world.

As you go, glorify God.

(BASED ON MATTHEW 5:13-14)

INVITING IN (recite together)

Lord, you are our refuge,
our strength, and our help.

TEACH US TO STOP STRIVING,

To be still & know
That you are God.

You will be exalted
AMONG THE NATIONS;
You will be exalted
IN THE EARTH.

(BASED ON PSALMS 46:1, 10)

INWARD PRAYER (10 minutes)

Read individually

> Search me, God, and know my heart; test me and know my anxious thoughts. See if there is any offensive way in me, and lead me in the way everlasting. (Psalms 139:23, 24).

Silence

Confession & Accountability

How am I? What struggles am I facing today?

What is God's truth in the midst of this struggle?

Is there anything in my life that is creating a barrier between me and God or between me and a person in my life? If so, what should I do about it?

Reflect on God's forgiveness. Thank God for the help He is ready to give.

WORSHIP (15 minutes)

Sing together

Communion

WORD (10 minutes)

Read out loud together

> BIBLE STORY: King David's sin and repentance (2 Sam. 11:1–12:25; Psalm 51)

> BIBLE TEACHING: Repent and believe (1 John 1:5–2:2)

RESPONSE (25 minutes)

Respond to the Word as a group or in pairs

What is God depositing IN your heart and mind through these Scriptures?

- *How would you summarize these passages?*

- *What is the key verse?*

- *What is the Lord teaching you through these passages?*

How can you conform to the image of Christ by living this OUT?

- *What attitude or way of thinking do I need to change?*

- *What action do I need to take?*

- *How will I do this? When will I do this?*

- *Who will keep me accountable?*

As you live this out, how will you express Jesus to those AROUND you?

- *How can I use these passages to tell someone about Jesus?*

- *Who will I share this with this week?*

- *As practice, rewrite or re-tell your summary of these passages and explain how they help you know Jesus.*

OUTWARD PRAYER (30 minutes)

Pray for each other

Pray for the people with whom you'll share

Pray for the Silk Road UPG on the following page

UNREACHED
PEOPLE
GROUP: *Pashtun*

O ne evening I struck up a conversation with a man named Sultan. When I went home that evening I immediately told my wife, "Honey, I met this man. As I was talking to him, I just felt this sense of peace," to which she replied, "Well, go back and meet with him again!" So, I went back to Sultan's shop and began talking to him again.

The peace that I felt transitioned into one of those Spirit-promptings to boldly and clearly explain the gospel.

Now we say in Afghanistan that an evangelist has about a 15-minute life span. Here's the scenario: I share about Jesus and then he kills me. The police arrive and ask, "What happened?" He responds, "Oh, this man was proselytizing," to which the police reply, "Well, let his body rot here so all can see what happens to those who try to convert a Muslim. Case closed." But I knew the Lord was telling me to do this, so I took a step of faith. In the Afghan language I said, "My God is my Father." Now, I just distanced myself from Islam because I said that I have a relationship with God, like a child to a parent, whereas Muslims find this idea of intimacy with God offensive. Allah is the master; they are his slaves. Because I said this, Sultan would be legally permitted to kill me. Instead, he gave a big smile and nodded his head. So, I took another step of faith and I said to Sultan, "My God's Son is Jesus." He smiled again and said, "Yes, He is." I was about ready to pass out. "Who are you?" I thought. He told me his story:

I am a religious man from a religious family. All the men in my family have been imams, they have been mullahs. I have been trained in the mosque, in the madrasah [Quranic school] since I was a young boy. One night I had a dream. I was walking to the madrasah, and there was a big storm. Every step I took there was lightning and thunder. It prevented me from getting to the madrasah. So I turned, and I met a lady who points into a room. In this room is a man standing full of glory. Then I wake up from my dream. It's my time to go to the madrasah, but on my way, there's no lightning, no thunder. I go in. I sit down with my teacher and explain to him the dream that I had the night before. My teacher looks at me and says, "You're unclean. Don't ever come back here again." I just lost my job, my career, my identity. I wondered, "Who was this man full of glory?" Well, I met a missionary, and this missionary began to teach me from his Holy Book. He began to teach me about Jesus, the Man full of glory. I gave my life to this Jesus. This missionary brought me into this small group of five other believers. The missionary met with us once a week and taught from the Holy Book. One week we're waiting for the missionary, but he never came. Later we found out he was shot and killed for sharing his faith

47

with us. Me and the other five guys ran for our lives. It's been nine months since I've read from the Holy Book or spoken to another believer—and now you're standing in front of me.

God led me to talk to Sultan. I brought him into my home, fed him, prayed with him, and read the Scripture with him. I brought him into the small group of believers I was working with. He was baptized and filled with the Holy Spirit. He began writing beautiful poetry and is now a great blessing to Pashtun believers throughout Afghanistan.

The Holy Spirit

As the Spirit fills us, His power overflows into every area of our lives, affecting all we think, say, and do. The Spirit equips us with supernatural gifts to fulfill our mission. We boldly proclaim Jesus everywhere to everyone, believing miraculous signs will follow. We regularly pray in the Spirit and exercise all the authority afforded to believers in Jesus' name. We affirm our wholehearted dependence on the Holy Spirit.

PRAY that missionaries will will commit themselves to relying on the Holy Spirit in everything they do.

PRAY that Pashtun believers will be filled with the Holy Spirit in the same way that the early believers of the church were, despite overt hostility against them.

PRAY for the nearly 44,300,000 Pashtun consisting of 60 distinct tribes found mainly in Afghanistan and Pakistan.

SENDING OUT (read by host)

YOU ARE THE

salt of the Earth

YOU ARE THE

light of the world.

As you go, glorify God.

(BASED ON MATTHEW 5:13-14)

INVITING IN (recite together)

*Lord, you are our refuge,
our strength, and our help.*

TEACH US TO STOP STRIVING,

To be still & know
That you are God.

You will be exalted

AMONG THE NATIONS;

You will be exalted

IN THE EARTH.

(BASED ON PSALMS 46:1, 10)

INWARD PRAYER (10 minutes)

Read individually

> Search me, God, and know my heart; test me and know my anxious thoughts. See if there is any offensive way in me, and lead me in the way everlasting. (Psalms 139:23, 24).

Silence

Confession & Accountability

How am I? What struggles am I facing today?

What is God's truth in the midst of this struggle?

Is there anything in my life that is creating a barrier between me and God or between me and a person in my life? If so, what should I do about it?

Reflect on God's forgiveness. Thank God for the help He is ready to give.

WORSHIP (15 minutes)

Sing together

Communion

WORD (10 minutes)

Read out loud together

BIBLE STORY: John the Baptizer prepares the way for Jesus (Luke 1:5-25, 57-80; Luke 3:1-22)

BIBLE TEACHING: Die to sin and be raised to life in Christ (Romans 6:1-11)

RESPONSE (25 minutes)

Respond to the Word as a group or in pairs

What is God depositing IN your heart and mind through these Scriptures?

- *How would you summarize these passages?*

- *What is the key verse?*

- *What is the Lord teaching you through these passages?*

How can you conform to the image of Christ by living this OUT?

- *What attitude or way of thinking do I need to change?*

- *What action do I need to take?*

- *How will I do this? When will I do this?*

- *Who will keep me accountable?*

As you live this out, how will you express Jesus to those AROUND you?

- *How can I use these passages to tell someone about Jesus?*

- *Who will I share this with this week?*

- *As practice, rewrite or re-tell your summary of these passages and explain how they help you know Jesus.*

OUTWARD PRAYER (30 minutes)

Pray for each other

Pray for the people with whom you'll share

Pray for the Silk Road UPG on the following page

Yagnobi

Ever dream of hiking into a valley lost in time, one that still appears very much the same as it did hundreds of years earlier? The Yagnob Valley is such a place and is home to the unreached people group called the Yagnobi. Their houses, lifestyle, and celebrations are a snapshot of the past. The Yagnobi are descendants of the ancient Sogdian people; they were isolated from Arab conquerors due to the remoteness of the Yagnob Valley. The Yagnobi language is somewhat of a relic, considered to be the closest thing to the original Sogdian language of northeastern Persia.

Gradually, the Yagnobi were pressured to convert to Islam, and today there are no known followers of Jesus among them. Like the intense terrain of their homeland, the Yagnobi are intense in their Muslim identity and in the spiritism that permeates their lives. Some of the most famous fortunetellers and witchdoctors in Tajikistan are Yagnobi. Despite the Soviet Union's attempts to destroy their identity, the Yagnobi people remain proud of their heritage.

Malika is an elderly lady who cooks lunch at my office. She loves to cook for us, to laugh, and to tell us that she is Yagnobi. In fact, if you ask her about being Yagnobi, she will tell you that she is a descendant of a Yagnobi king. Malika has actually never set foot in the Yagnob Valley because her parents were forcefully relocated to work on cotton plantations. Malika dreams of returning to her people's homeland before she dies. I hope to be a part of that great homecoming for Malika— and another homecoming, the one of the Yagnobi people knowing, loving, and taking pride in worshiping Jesus as they were created to do.

Learning

An attitude of lifelong learning helps missionaries understand the culture and worldview of those with whom they work.

PRAY that missionaries will be committed to ask good questions and continually learn from the people they are trying to reach for the sake of representing the gospel in the most culturally respectful and relevant way.

PRAY that Tajik followers of Jesus would catch the vision to reach out to their near-neighbors, the Yagnobi, to see faith grow and the church planted among every ethnicity in and around their country.

PRAY for the 16,000 Yagnobi-speaking Yagnobi found only in Tajikistan, of which there are no known believers.

SENDING OUT (read by host)

YOU ARE THE

salt of the Earth

YOU ARE THE

light of the world.

As you go, glorify God.

(BASED ON MATTHEW 5:13-14)

Week 5

INVITING IN (recite together)

*Lord, you are our refuge,
our strength, and our help.*

TEACH US TO STOP STRIVING,

To be still & know
That you are God.

You will be exalted
AMONG THE NATIONS;
You will be exalted
IN THE EARTH.

(BASED ON PSALMS 46:1, 10)

INWARD PRAYER (10 minutes)

Read individually

> Search me, God, and know my heart; test me and know my anxious thoughts. See if there is any offensive way in me, and lead me in the way everlasting. (Psalms 139:23, 24).

Silence

Confession & Accountability

How am I? What struggles am I facing today?

What is God's truth in the midst of this struggle?

Is there anything in my life that is creating a barrier between me and God or between me and a person in my life? If so, what should I do about it?

Reflect on God's forgiveness. Thank God for the help He is ready to give.

WORSHIP (15 minutes)

Sing together

Communion

WORD (10 minutes)

Read out loud together

> **BIBLE STORY:** Jesus' call to follow Him (Luke 5:1-11; 27-32)
>
> **BIBLE TEACHING:** Abide in Christ (John 15:1–17)

RESPONSE (25 minutes)

Respond to the Word as a group or in pairs

What is God depositing IN your heart and mind through these Scriptures?

- *How would you summarize these passages?*

- *What is the key verse?*

- *What is the Lord teaching you through these passages?*

How can you conform to the image of Christ by living this OUT?

- *What attitude or way of thinking do I need to change?*

- *What action do I need to take?*

- *How will I do this? When will I do this?*

- *Who will keep me accountable?*

As you live this out, how will you express Jesus to those AROUND you?

- *How can I use these passages to tell someone about Jesus?*

- *Who will I share this with this week?*

- *As practice, rewrite or re-tell your summary of these passages and explain how they help you know Jesus.*

OUTWARD PRAYER (30 minutes)

Pray for each other

Pray for the people with whom you'll share

Pray for the Silk Road UPG on the following page

UNREACHED
PEOPLE
GROUP: *Nuristani*

I n the summer of 2010, a team of skilled relief workers was assembled to take an
arduous trek deep into the Hindu Kush mountains of northern Afghanistan. Their
destination was a valley hidden from modern civilization, home of the Nuristani.
This region was once known as Kafiristan, Land of the Infidels, during a time when
the Nuristani people practiced Buddhism. In 1895, the Nuristani converted to Islam

and remain Muslim today. The team of ten workers from around the world planned to do medical eye work and "be the hands and feet of Jesus." Two of the team members were my friends who had been living in Afghanistan for over thirty years by this time. The team was excited about this trip, though fully aware of the dangers they faced. The roads to Nuristan only went so far, and the remainder of the journey would be on foot with horses to carry supplies. On August 8, as the team members arrived at their vehicles, returning from this successful medical outreach, they were met by members of the Taliban and all ten were shot and killed.

Acts of service and love were done in Jesus' name, lives given and blood spilled in an effort to bring the Nuristani people the salvation message of Jesus. Who will pray open the doors and return to these hidden tribes to see His Kingdom established? Who will obey the directive of our Lord to reach every tribe?

Pioneering

Living and proclaiming the gospel in a culturally appropriate manner among unreached people groups with the goal of planting the church where it does not exist.

PRAY that missionaries would have the creativity, persistence, and spiritual depth to plant the church in places that are hard to reach.

PRAY that the few believers in Afghanistan will have the courage and endurance to reach out to their near-neighbors, the Nuristani, and invite them to follow Jesus.

PRAY for the roughly 250,000 Nuristani in northeastern Afghanistan of which there are zero known believers and no access to Christian witness.

YOU ARE THE
salt of the Earth
YOU ARE THE
light of the world.
As you go, glorify God.

(BASED ON MATTHEW 5:13-14)

INVITING IN (recite together)

Lord, you are our refuge,
our strength, and our help.

TEACH US TO STOP STRIVING,

To be still & know
that you are God.

You will be exalted
AMONG THE NATIONS;
You will be exalted
IN THE EARTH.

(BASED ON PSALMS 46:1, 10)

INWARD PRAYER (10 minutes)

Read individually

> Search me, God, and know my heart; test me and know my anxious thoughts. See if there is any offensive way in me, and lead me in the way everlasting. (Psalms 139:23, 24).

Silence

Confession & Accountability

How am I? What struggles am I facing today?

What is God's truth in the midst of this struggle?

Is there anything in my life that is creating a barrier between me and God or between me and a person in my life? If so, what should I do about it?

Reflect on God's forgiveness. Thank God for the help He is ready to give.

WORSHIP (15 minutes)

Sing together

Communion

WORD (10 minutes)

Read out loud together

> **BIBLE STORY:** Jesus' authority over the spiritual and physical world
> (Luke 8:22–56)

> **BIBLE TEACHING:** Pray in the authority of Jesus' name (John 14:1–14)

RESPONSE (25 minutes)

Respond to the Word as a group or in pairs

What is God depositing IN your heart and mind through these Scriptures?

- *How would you summarize these passages?*

- *What is the key verse?*

- *What is the Lord teaching you through these passages?*

How can you conform to the image of Christ by living this OUT?

- *What attitude or way of thinking do I need to change?*

- *What action do I need to take?*

- *How will I do this? When will I do this?*

- *Who will keep me accountable?*

As you live this out, how will you express Jesus to those AROUND you?

- *How can I use these passages to tell someone about Jesus?*

- *Who will I share this with this week?*

- *As practice, rewrite or re-tell your summary of these passages and explain how they help you know Jesus.*

OUTWARD PRAYER (30 minutes)

Pray for each other

Pray for the people with whom you'll share

Pray for the Silk Road UPG on the following page

UNENGAGED UNREACHED PEOPLE GROUP: *Shina*

There is no story for this people group. No one from our movement has had an experience with a person from this people group. Not only that, there is currently not a single known missionary from any organization involved in church planting among this people group. They are not only unreached, they are unengaged.

In the Silk Road, the places we find these people groups are called "Zero Zones," in other words, a region that has no known believers, likely no complete Bible translation or recording in this people group's heart language, no known churches, and no known missionaries living in and focusing on evangelism and church planting among the indigenous people of that region.

The data for unengaged unreached people groups (UUPGs) are dynamic, constantly changing with the ebb and flow of your prayerful awareness, missionary movement, obstacles that impede the work being done in some places, and the doors God supernaturally opens in others.

There is no guarantee that at the moment you read this, this people group remains in a Zero Zone, but what can be safely said is that many Zero Zones remain. Entire ethno-linguistic blocks may be still hidden from the radar or threaten too high a risk or for a myriad of other reasons continue to be unengaged. Pray for them all—the ones whose names you can't pronounce, the ones whose names you have yet to hear, the ones whom God is putting on your heart to reach out to with the beautiful message of Jesus.

"For, 'Everyone who calls on the name of the Lord will be saved.' How, then, can they call on the one they have not believed in? And how can they believe in the one of whom they have not heard? And how can they hear without someone preaching to them? And how can anyone preach unless they are sent? As it is written: 'How beautiful are the feet of those who bring good news!'" (Rom. 10:13–15)

Apostolic Function

A lens worn by every one of our missionaries that sees his or her calling as part of God's plan to reach every tribe, tongue, and people. It places a focus on proclaiming the gospel to unreached people groups, planting the church among them, and raising up participants in God's global mission. It compels the whole church to take the whole gospel to the whole world.

PRAY that as missionaries focus on planting the church among every people group, they will have the discernment to distinguish between distractions, merely good endeavors, and the Spirit-led pursuits that drive forward the spread of the gospel and lay the groundwork for the church in places that do not yet have any believers, Bibles, communities of faith, or church planting teams.

PRAY that God puts a vision in the hearts of MBBs that neighbor these unengaged unreached people groups to boldly, lovingly, and wisely engage these communities with the gospel.

PRAY for the 755,000 Shina of Pakistan and Afghanistan along with the estimated 3,207 unengaged unengaged unreached people groups (many of which are scattered throughout the Silk Road) that exist without an indigenous community of Jesus followers or a single boots-on-the-ground church planting team present to bring them the good news.

SENDING OUT (read by host)

YOU ARE THE

salt of the Earth

YOU ARE THE

light of the world.

As you go, glorify God.

(BASED ON MATTHEW 5:13-14)

INVITING IN (recite together)

Lord, you are our refuge,
our strength, and our help.

TEACH US TO STOP STRIVING,

To be still & know
that you are God.

You will be exalted
AMONG THE NATIONS;
You will be exalted
IN THE EARTH.

(BASED ON PSALMS 46:1, 10)

INWARD PRAYER (10 minutes)

Read individually

>Search me, God, and know my heart; test me and know my anxious thoughts. See if there is any offensive way in me, and lead me in the way everlasting. (Psalms 139:23, 24).

Silence

Confession & Accountability

How am I? What struggles am I facing today?

What is God's truth in the midst of this struggle?

Is there anything in my life that is creating a barrier between me and God or between me and a person in my life? If so, what should I do about it?

Reflect on God's forgiveness. Thank God for the help He is ready to give.

WORSHIP (15 minutes)

Sing together

Communion

WORD (10 minutes)

Read out loud together

> **BIBLE STORY:** Jesus and His followers' last supper before the crucifixion (Luke 22:1-23)
>
> **BIBLE TEACHING:** Make meeting with believers a priority (Heb. 10:19–25)

RESPONSE (25 minutes)

Respond to the Word as a group or in pairs

What is God depositing IN your heart and mind through these Scriptures?

- *How would you summarize these passages?*

- *What is the key verse?*

LIVE DEAD TOGETHER: A PRACTICE IN GROUP ABIDING

- *What is the Lord teaching you through these passages?*

How can you conform to the image of Christ by living this OUT?

- *What attitude or way of thinking do I need to change?*

- *What action do I need to take?*

- *How will I do this? When will I do this?*

- *Who will keep me accountable?*

As you live this out, how will you express Jesus to those AROUND you?

- *How can I use these passages to tell someone about Jesus?*

- *Who will I share this with this week?*

- *As practice, rewrite or re-tell your summary of these passages and explain how they help you know Jesus.*

OUTWARD PRAYER (30 minutes)

Pray for each other

Pray for the people with whom you'll share

Pray for the Silk Road UPG on the following page

Central Eurasian Russian[3]

A nation living among another nation in a place where ethnicity determines your worth as a person. I'm Russian, and my ethnicity is what defines me. I can hardly call myself Kyrgyz because to be called Kyrgyz, I had to be born Kyrgyz. I grew up in a nation that only now can I call my own. My whole childhood I saw only our differences in culture, customs, and beliefs. My nationality has no power to determine my affiliation with my people and thousands like me.

We were born "not in our country." Our values and beliefs are a mix of Russian, Kyrgyz, and other cultures living in the neighborhood. We celebrate Russian holidays as well as Kyrgyz. We get off school and work for both Ramadan and Russian Easter. On both holidays kids walk around and sing songs, asking for sweets or colored eggs. We learn to respect each other and often say good things to each other during those days. On Ramadan I write a message to my Kyrgyz friend, and on Easter she writes me. But everything has become mixed up over the past few decades, which makes it difficult for people to understand who they are and to what people they can relate.

I would call the Russians of Central Eurasia the people in search of themselves and their belonging. This search in many respects explains the huge flow of migration of the Russian-speaking population to the territory of Russia. The generation that grew up after the collapse of the USSR has no religious ties—some are nominal Orthodox Christians, many are atheist. They believe in themselves most of the time. Yet I think they seek something bigger than they are and something better for their lives, especially now that the government gives them few opportunities for life.

From my experience, Russians that genuinely follow Jesus have a vision for Kyrgyz people to come to faith. Of course, they have cultural barriers and some fear and prejudice, but I think these barriers will fall if we pray seriously about it and talk about it in our churches. Russian Protestants can be a connection between missionaries from the West and the indigenous peoples in the Central Eurasian countries. I can say about myself that I understand Western workers because of my worldview and I understand Kyrgyz people and their worldview. I believe that the church is a place for all nations, different nations, and these distinctions bring beauty in the church.

[3]Although Russians in Central Eurasia are not "unreached," they represent a vast population of people that are superficially or minimally reached. Not only does our apostolic lens lead us to reach out for the sake of their eternal destiny, but it also sees the potential for partnership with Russian believers for the gospel to ripple out to the unreached peoples along the Silk Road.

Partnering

We seek relationship between missionaries and the indigenous churches we plant. Developing self-governing, self-supporting, and self-propagating churches is foundational to the relationship. Fruitful ministry occurs when the mission and the national church serve together in humility.

PRAY for missionaries who work among the peoples of the Silk Road. Pray that God will open their hearts to a wide variety of people and nationalities, that their hearts may be ready to serve them, regardless of their faces, as true servants to these peoples.

PRAY for Russian-speaking churches to open their doors to people from other cultures, to accept these people and learn to see them just as Christ sees them. Pray for courage and boldness to go from their churches into the streets and to talk to people about God, regardless of persecution from communities and the government.

PRAY that the gospel will be clearly revealed to the hearts of the approximately 4.8 million Russians spread across the Silk Road.

SENDING OUT (read by host)

YOU ARE THE
salt of the Earth
YOU ARE THE
light of the world.

As you go, glorify God.

(BASED ON MATTHEW 5:13-14)

INVITING IN (recite together)

Lord, you are our refuge,
our strength, and our help.

TEACH US TO STOP STRIVING,

To be still & know
That you are God.

You will be exalted

AMONG THE NATIONS;

You will be exalted

IN THE EARTH.

(BASED ON PSALMS 46:1, 10)

INWARD PRAYER (10 minutes)

Read individually

> Search me, God, and know my heart; test me and know my anxious thoughts. See if there is any offensive way in me, and lead me in the way everlasting. (Psalms 139:23, 24).

Silence

Confession & Accountability

How am I? What struggles am I facing today?

What is God's truth in the midst of this struggle?

Is there anything in my life that is creating a barrier between me and God or between me and a person in my life? If so, what should I do about it?

Reflect on God's forgiveness. Thank God for the help He is ready to give.

WORSHIP (15 minutes)

Sing together

Communion

WORD (10 minutes)

Read out loud together

    BIBLE STORY: Jesus' followers baptized with the Holy Spirit
        (Acts 2:1–42)

    BIBLE TEACHING: The Holy Spirit is at work in you (John 14:15-27)

RESPONSE (25 minutes)

Respond to the Word as a group or in pairs

What is God depositing IN your heart and mind through these Scriptures?

- *How would you summarize these passages?*

- *What is the key verse?*

- *What is the Lord teaching you through these passages?*

How can you conform to the image of Christ by living this OUT?

- *What attitude or way of thinking do I need to change?*

- *What action do I need to take?*

- *How will I do this? When will I do this?*

- *Who will keep me accountable?*

As you live this out, how will you express Jesus to those AROUND you?

- *How can I use these passages to tell someone about Jesus?*

- *Who will I share this with this week?*

- *As practice, rewrite or re-tell your summary of these passages and explain how they help you know Jesus.*

OUTWARD PRAYER (30 minutes)

Pray for each other

Pray for the people with whom you'll share

Pray for the Silk Road UPG on the following page

UNREACHED PEOPLE GROUP: Kyrgyz

Just two brisk winter days before Christmas, a Kyrgyz friend asked me to share the Christmas story at the English conversation club he teaches. This was an amazing opportunity to tell Kyrgyz students the true story of Christmas, something certainly none of them had ever heard. I would have liked more time to put together a truly good "storied" version of Luke 1 and

2, but time was not on my side, so I decided to read the story directly from the text and pray for the best.

Even though our new teammates had not been in the country long enough to be able to share in the presentation of the gospel that day, they were fully equipped to pray. One teammate came with me and the rest stayed at home, interceding for the students, for a move of the Holy Spirit, and for God's will to be accomplished in this key moment.

The time for my 10-minute Christmas presentation arrived all too soon. Halfway through, I realized I never opened my Bible. Every word I said was not my own, but the Holy Spirit's. He spoke through me to these Kyrgyz students, and they hung on every word! When I explained Emmanuel, God with us, their eyes were as big as saucers and their mouths hung open. "Wow, God is with us!" was repeated again and again by each one. Their worldview was shattered because they grew up with Islam which implies that God is never with us.

At the end many students thanked me, but one female student stood out. She said to me, "Thank you for this amazing story. It's awesome. I'm going to tell everyone I know because everyone needs to hear this story!" My team and I couldn't agree more.

Teams

Collections of people working together for the common goal of planting the church among unreached peoples. Teams are empowered to create and to define a team structure according to their context.

PRAY that missionary teams will work for unity in vision and relationship with one another so as to enhance rather than distract from the goal of planting the church among the unreached.

PRAY for the struggling Kyrgyz church to be encouraged and empowered to be a light.

PRAY for the roughly 4,800,000 Kyrgyz of Kyrgyzstan who need to know that God is with us.

SENDING OUT (read by host)

YOU ARE THE
salt of the Earth
YOU ARE THE
light of the world.

As you go, glorify God.

(BASED ON MATTHEW 5:13-14)

INVITING IN (recite together)

Lord, you are our refuge,
our strength, and our help.

TEACH US TO STOP STRIVING,

To be still & know
That you are God.

You will be exalted
AMONG THE NATIONS;
You will be exalted
IN THE EARTH.

(BASED ON PSALMS 46:1, 10)

INWARD PRAYER (10 minutes)

Read individually

> Search me, God, and know my heart; test me and know my anxious thoughts. See if there is any offensive way in me, and lead me in the way everlasting. (Psalms 139:23, 24).

Silence

Confession & Accountability

How am I? What struggles am I facing today?

What is God's truth in the midst of this struggle?

Is there anything in my life that is creating a barrier between me and God or between me and a person in my life? If so, what should I do about it?

Reflect on God's forgiveness. Thank God for the help He is ready to give.

WORSHIP (15 minutes)

Sing together

Communion

WORD (10 minutes)

Read out loud together

> **BIBLE STORY:** The martyrdom of Stephen (Acts 6:8–8:3)
>
> **BIBLE TEACHING:** Endure persecution. Jesus is worth it (Romans 8:1–39)

RESPONSE (25 minutes)

Respond to the Word as a group or in pairs

What is God depositing IN your heart and mind through these Scriptures?

- *How would you summarize these passages?*

- *What is the key verse?*

- *What is the Lord teaching you through these passages?*

How can you conform to the image of Christ by living this OUT?

- *What attitude or way of thinking do I need to change?*

- *What action do I need to take?*

- *How will I do this? When will I do this?*

- *Who will keep me accountable?*

As you live this out, how will you express Jesus to those AROUND you?

- *How can I use these passages to tell someone about Jesus?*

- *Who will I share this with this week?*

- *As practice, rewrite or re-tell your summary of these passages and explain how they help you know Jesus.*

OUTWARD PRAYER (30 minutes)

Pray for each other

Pray for the people with whom you'll share

Pray for the Silk Road UPG on the following page

UNREACHED PEOPLE GROUP: *Azerbaijani*

Murad and I sat on a bench along the shore of the Caspian Sea, taking in the aroma of its salty blue water mingled with the freshly brewed Azerchai that gently warmed our hands. As we talked about the meaning of life, I enjoyed the scenery but noticed Murad's mind was occupied with places beyond what our eyes saw in that present moment.

Murad is a bright young man who recently graduated from a local university but struggled to find a job. He depends on the income of his family members and is unable to collect enough money to marry his fiancée. After world oil prices fell, the local currency devalued and many businesses closed, leaving young people with little hope to join the workforce. Overwhelmed by this, he and many other young Azerbaijani men like him are anxious to leave the country, and Murad continues to ask my advice on how to do that. He is convinced the prosperity of the West will fill him with hope and give him the joy that he seeks.

Pray with us that Murad and the young people of Azerbaijan would awaken to the real reason their hearts are restless and without hope. Pray they would pursue the Giver of Life and become a light to their nation.

Transformation

Transformation is a change from a contrary condition of human existence to God's purposes to a condition in which people are able to enjoy fullness of life in harmony with God. Every activity will be regarded as an opportunity to touch people in love, to speak relevant words of truth pointing them to God, and to experience the supernatural intervention of the Holy Spirit.

PRAY that missionaries will have the linguistic ability and Spirit-led words to speak into the lives of those to whom they reach out.

PRAY that the small group of Azeri believers would reflect the transformation that only Christ can bring.

PRAY for the nearly 8,850,000 Azerbaijani of Azerbaijan, plus over 20,000,000 ethnic Azeri scattered throughout the globe, that desperately need a message of hope.

SENDING OUT (read by host)

YOU ARE THE

salt of the Earth

YOU ARE THE

light of the world.

As you go, glorify God.

(BASED ON MATTHEW 5:13-14)

INVITING IN (recite together)

*Lord, you are our refuge,
our strength, and our help.*
TEACH US TO STOP STRIVING,

To be still & know
That you are God.

You will be exalted
AMONG THE NATIONS;
You will be exalted
IN THE EARTH.

(BASED ON PSALMS 46:1, 10)

INWARD PRAYER (10 minutes)

Read individually

> Search me, God, and know my heart; test me and know my anxious thoughts. See if there is any offensive way in me, and lead me in the way everlasting. (Psalms 139:23, 24).

Silence

Confession & Accountability

How am I? What struggles am I facing today?

What is God's truth in the midst of this struggle?

Is there anything in my life that is creating a barrier between me and God or between me and a person in my life? If so, what should I do about it?

Reflect on God's forgiveness. Thank God for the help He is ready to give.

WORSHIP (15 minutes)

Sing together

Communion

WORD (10 minutes)

Read out loud together

    BIBLE STORY: Paul's missionary journey to Macedonia and Corinth
        (Acts 16:4–40; 18:1–11)

    BIBLE TEACHING: Spread the good news (2 Cor. 5:11–6:13)

RESPONSE (25 minutes)

Respond to the Word as a group or in pairs

What is God depositing IN your heart and mind through these Scriptures?

- *How would you summarize these passages?*

- *What is the key verse?*

- *What is the Lord teaching you through these passages?*

How can you conform to the image of Christ by living this OUT?

- *What attitude or way of thinking do I need to change?*

- *What action do I need to take?*

- *How will I do this? When will I do this?*

- *Who will keep me accountable?*

As you live this out, how will you express Jesus to those AROUND you?

- *How can I use these passages to tell someone about Jesus?*

- *Who will I share this with this week?*

- *As practice, rewrite or re-tell your summary of these passages and explain how they help you know Jesus.*

OUTWARD PRAYER (30 minutes)

Pray for each other

Pray for the people with whom you'll share

Pray for the Silk Road UPG on the following page

UNREACHED PEOPLE GROUP: *Gujjar*

Nine-year-old Ahmed smiled as he carefully unpacked the boxes. The Christian foreigner invited him, along with his six-year-old cousin, to help decorate her home for Christmas. As the boys wrapped the lights around the artificial tree, they gazed in wonder. "What is this all about?" they asked.

The pale-skinned lady adjusted her headscarf to keep it in place and joyfully said, "It's for Christmas!" There was an awkward silence as the boys stared at her in confusion. "You know Christmas?" The boys shook their heads. "It's the day we celebrate the birth of Isa al Mesih. You know Isa al Mesih, right?" More silence. She continued, "You know, Isa al Mesih from the Injil [Gospels or New Testament]? 'The Son of Maryam.' Haven't you ever heard the imam talk about the Prophet Isa from the Koran?" The boys shook their heads and looked at one another in confusion. "Are you telling me that you have never in your life heard the name of Isa before?" Ahmed shook his head, "No. Never."

Now she was the one without words. The reality of the state of lostness for this family and the entire Gujjar-Pathan tribe pierced her heart deeply. How is it that someone can grow up, live their lives, and never hear the name of Jesus?

As they unpacked the nativity scene, the lady used the figurines to recount the story of the birth of the Savior. The boys looked at each other and giggled. It was a new and different kind of story—a story of wonder. Life circumstances led these boys back to their remote villages, but the prayer of this foreign visitor continues to be that the words of the Christmas story will reverberate in the hearts of those now young men. May someone take the good news of Jesus to their village where it has yet to be proclaimed.

Community

We will integrate our lives with neighbors and indigenous believers. A logical outgrowth of commitment to local language, to learning culture, and to lifestyle evangelism is living where we minister.

PRAY that missionaries will branch out of the comfort zone of their own culture for the sake of living and speaking the gospel among the people God has led them to live.

PRAY that Gujjar believers stay committed to staying in their home villages, despite the social pressure against them for following Jesus, for the sake of reaching their communities with the good news.

PRAY that the name of Jesus will be made famous among the over two million Gujjar of Pakistan.

SENDING OUT (read by host)

YOU ARE THE

salt of the Earth

YOU ARE THE

light of the world.

As you go, glorify God.

(BASED ON MATTHEW 5:13-14)

INVITING IN (recite together)

Lord, you are our refuge,
our strength, and our help.

TEACH US TO STOP STRIVING,

To be still & know
That you are God.

You will be exalted
AMONG THE NATIONS;
You will be exalted
IN THE EARTH.

(BASED ON PSALMS 46:1, 10)

INWARD PRAYER (10 minutes)

Read individually

> Search me, God, and know my heart; test me and know my anxious thoughts. See if there is any offensive way in me, and lead me in the way everlasting. (Psalms 139:23, 24).

Silence

Confession & Accountability

How am I? What struggles am I facing today?

What is God's truth in the midst of this struggle?

Is there anything in my life that is creating a barrier between me and God or between me and a person in my life? If so, what should I do about it?

Reflect on God's forgiveness. Thank God for the help He is ready to give.

WORSHIP (15 minutes)

Sing together

Communion

WORD (10 minutes)

Read out loud together

> **BIBLE STORY:** The body of Christ (1 Cor. 12:4–13:13)
>
> **BIBLE TEACHING:** Build the church (Eph. 4:1–32)

RESPONSE (25 minutes)

Respond to the Word as a group or in pairs

What is God depositing IN your heart and mind through these Scriptures?

- *How would you summarize these passages?*

- *What is the key verse?*

- *What is the Lord teaching you through these passages?*

How can you conform to the image of Christ by living this OUT?

- *What attitude or way of thinking do I need to change?*

- *What action do I need to take?*

- *How will I do this? When will I do this?*

- *Who will keep me accountable?*

As you live this out, how will you express Jesus to those AROUND you?

- *How can I use these passages to tell someone about Jesus?*

- *Who will I share this with this week?*

- *As practice, rewrite or re-tell your summary of these passages and explain how they help you know Jesus.*

OUTWARD PRAYER (30 minutes)

Pray for each other

Pray for the people with whom you'll share

Pray for the Silk Road UPG on the following page

UNREACHED
PEOPLE
GROUP: Uzbek

An Uzbek coworker and friend shared with me that his church small group wanted to reach out to the tuberculosis hospital in town and start small groups for its patients. Tuberculosis was still a major killer in this part of the world, and people often traveled from outlying regions to the capital to receive medical treatment at this particular hospital. The conditions of hospitals such as this in Uzbekistan were poor, at best, and often their directors would keep doors shut tightly to outsiders in an effort to hide their dereliction. Even family members of tuberculosis patients were not allowed inside. Instead, they stood outside under the open windows of the hospital, rain or shine, waiting to provide the medication and food their ill family member required, necessary supplies the hospital itself did not provide. The sick patient would lower a basket on a string and then haul up the goods their parent our spouse brought, along with any other news or tokens for which they might be waiting.

This small group of believers knew prayer was essential if they were going to see their impossible dream come true. Each week they met for prayer in front of the tuberculosis hospital at 4 a.m., which allowed everyone to arrive at work on time or at home to see children off to school afterward. For four weeks, they met in the dark, early morning hours to circle the hospital and pray for healing, salvation, and open doors. As Christmas approached, they gathered their courage to approach the hospital director to see if she would allow them to bring fruits and sweets into the hospital for the patients as a Christmas outreach, treats they would pay for from their meager incomes. They could barely believe it when she agreed!

The Christmas outreach was a success, and the small group continued to come to the hospital to share Christ. Eventually, their outreaches progressed to a church service. Their weekly offering bought medications for some of the patients, and some of the patients began to make decisions to follow Jesus. One patient was Sergei. He was eager to learn about and soak up God's love and grace. Eventually, he began to lead one of the small groups that met during the week. It was like a beautiful flower blossoming amidst the rubble of a rundown hospital.

The time came for Sergei and two other patients who were also believers to return to their hometown about an 18-hour train ride away. I picked the three men up from the hospital and gave them a ride to the train station. The image of Sergei's face growing smaller and smaller as the train pulled away from the station is etched in my mind. Sergei never made it to his destination we were later told. Two police officers boarded the train for a passport inspection, and Sergei took the opportunity to share the gospel with them. The officers responded by taking him to a container car and beating him to death. His body was found several days later full of bruises and broken bones. Several weeks later his two fellow travelers were also martyred in their hometown as they shared their faith with others.

These men found hope in Jesus because a small group of believers sacrificed their time, money, and personal comfort to reach out. Truly following Jesus' steps, the church small group gave it all. Sergei and the other believers, knowing the threats in front of them, did as well. Though their stories met tragic ends, I still wonder how many families in those remote Uzbek villages have come to faith due to the willingness of those men to lay down their lives for Jesus.

Sacrifice

We recognize that the people groups that remain unreached face hostile spiritual and physical contexts of living. We commit ourselves to pay whatever price is necessary to reach them with the gospel.

PRAY for the spiritual grit and discernment that missionaries need to live and work in hostile environments.

PRAY that the indigenous church would have the courage and depth of faith to lead in the willingness to sacrifice everything for Jesus who sacrificed all for us.

PRAY that faith will blossom among the 24,200,000 Uzbek of Uzbekistan, along with those scattered across the Silk Road.

SENDING OUT (read by host)

YOU ARE THE

salt of the Earth

YOU ARE THE

light of the world.

As you go, glorify God.

(BASED ON MATTHEW 5:13-14)

INVITING IN (recite together)

*Lord, you are our refuge,
our strength, and our help.*

TEACH US TO STOP STRIVING,

To be still & know that you are God.

You will be exalted

AMONG THE NATIONS;

You will be exalted

IN THE EARTH.

(BASED ON PSALMS 46:1, 10)

INWARD PRAYER (10 minutes)

Read individually

> Search me, God, and know my heart; test me and know my anxious thoughts. See if there is any offensive way in me, and lead me in the way everlasting. (Psalms 139:23, 24).

Silence

Confession & Accountability

How am I? What struggles am I facing today?

What is God's truth in the midst of this struggle?

Is there anything in my life that is creating a barrier between me and God or between me and a person in my life? If so, what should I do about it?

Reflect on God's forgiveness. Thank God for the help He is ready to give.

WORSHIP (15 minutes)

Sing together

Communion

WORD (10 minutes)

Read out loud together

> **BIBLE STORY:** John's vision (Rev. 1:1–20)
>
> **BIBLE TEACHING:** Look forward to eternity in God's presence
> (Rev. 21:1–27)

RESPONSE (25 minutes)

Respond to the Word as a group or in pairs

What is God depositing IN your heart and mind through these Scriptures?

- *How would you summarize these passages?*

- *What is the key verse?*

- *What is the Lord teaching you through these passages?*

How can you conform to the image of Christ by living this OUT?

- *What attitude or way of thinking do I need to change?*

- *What action do I need to take?*

- *How will I do this? When will I do this?*

- *Who will keep me accountable?*

As you live this out, how will you express Jesus to those AROUND you?

- *How can I use these passages to tell someone about Jesus?*

- *Who will I share this with this week?*

- *As practice, rewrite or re-tell your summary of these passages and explain how they help you know Jesus.*

OUTWARD PRAYER (30 minutes)

Pray for each other

Pray for the people with whom you'll share

Pray for the Silk Road UPG on the following page

UNREACHED PEOPLE GROUP: *Turks*

Picnics at dusk, drums in the street, lethargic mornings, and irritable bus drivers are characteristics of Ramadan, the ritual fasting of all food, drink, and cigarettes during daylight hours for a specific month. Turks, secure in their identity as Muslims, are often nominal in practice, but most take advantage of this holy month to try to compensate for any impiety.

I will never forget our first Ramadan in Turkey. Our neighbor's daughter came down to ask us to help her with her English homework. She browsed our bookshelf and then seated herself on our couch to enjoy some conversation and my attempt at Turkish coffee. "I hate Ramadan," she confided. "It's hard. I'm tired all the time. Everyone is grouchy with each other. But I have to do it because I sin. I know that God is angry with me."

The fact that a sweet and fairly non-rebellious university student like Nur was so profoundly aware of her sin struck me like a dart. She felt the weight of her inability to reach God, and Islam's rituals provided no guarantee of rescue.

That realization drives us year by year to engage with Turks. It motivates us to sit through countless hours of bearing with our own linguistic incompetence, to continually come to terms with our own human frailty as we make cultural faux pas, to face rejection and mocking, and to work for the last decade of our lives believing there will be fruit while seeing very little. Add to this, the growing pains that come with working alongside other frail individuals as a church planting team. And yet, open accountability to team members and willing submission to leadership sharpens us, provides encouragement when we are weary, and extends our reach. If Nur finds freedom from sin and ritualism through Jesus, every painstaking effort will all be worth it.

Accountability

Authority is given by God and essential to who we are. We will respect, honor, and obey our authorities, considering them God's means of protection, counsel, and covering.

PRAY that missionaries will be willing to be held accountable to leaders and teammates for the sake of integrity and effectiveness in the pursuit of bringing the gospel to the unreached.

PRAY that indigenous believers will seek community and relationships of trust and accountability with one another.

PRAY for the 60,000,000 Turks of Turkey who, just like Nur, know deep down their sins cannot be compensated for by any amount of good works or religious effort.

SENDING OUT (read by host)

YOU ARE THE
salt of the Earth
YOU ARE THE
light of the world.

As you go, glorify God.

(BASED ON MATTHEW 5:13-14)

140

PART TWO

Building Communities of Faith

through responses to early church planting issues

with emphasis on *Live Dead Silk Road*

strategic commitments

Week 1

INVITING IN (recite together)

Lord, you are our refuge,
our strength, and our help.

TEACH US TO STOP STRIVING,

To be still & know
That you are God.

You will be exalted
AMONG THE NATIONS;
You will be exalted
IN THE EARTH.

(BASED ON PSALMS 46:1, 10)

INWARD PRAYER (10 minutes)

Read individually

> Search me, God, and know my heart; test me and know my anxious thoughts. See if there is any offensive way in me, and lead me in the way everlasting. (Psalms 139:23, 24).

Silence

Confession & Accountability

How am I? What struggles am I facing today?

What is God's truth in the midst of this struggle?

Is there anything in my life that is creating a barrier between me and God or between me and a person in my life? If so, what should I do about it?

Reflect on God's forgiveness. Thank God for the help He is ready to give.

WORSHIP (15 minutes)

Sing together

Communion

WORD (10 minutes)

Read out loud together

BIBLE STUDY: Church planting in Ephesus (Acts 18:24–20:1)

RESPONSE (25 minutes)

Respond to the Word as a group

What is God building IN our community through this Scripture?

- *What is the main point of this passage?*

- *How is this passage relevant to building communities of faith?*

- *What is the Lord teaching us through this passage?*

How can we mature as the body of Christ by living this OUT?

- *What elements of our church/small group's culture need growth/maturity?*

- *What part do each of us have to play to see the answer to the question above realized?*

- *How and when will we take action steps to do this?*

- *How will we keep each other accountable?*

How will we invest in those AROUND us to see more communities of faith in Jesus formed?

- *How will living this out help our community of faith better reflect Jesus to those around us?*

- *Who can we invite to discover Jesus with us?*

- *How will we actively work toward more communities of faith being formed?*

OUTWARD PRAYER (30 minutes)

Pray for each other

Pray for the people with whom you'll share

Pray for the Silk Road UPG on the following page

UNREACHED PEOPLE GROUP: *Lezgi*

Sayad was a girl in her late teens. Even though I met her at a women's gathering, she was quiet as every Lezgi girl was supposed to be. She was rocking a baby while trying to take care of her toddler. She had many questions, which she was afraid to voice. She knew that her every action was watched and talked about. Her life was supposed to line up with the expectations of her community. If it didn't, Sayad would feel the consequences—she would be cursed and kicked out of her husband's family. She would lose not only her status in the community and her livelihood, she would lose her children as well.

Sayad felt trapped. The world was changing, and the traditions of her people didn't provide the guidance to the issues she faced. She didn't dare disobey, but how could she wrestle with the reality of life if what the community prescribed did not satisfy her questions?

The Lezgi people as a whole struggle to preserve their identity in tradition, but what if, instead, they found their identity in the God who created them and made a beautiful redemption plan at His own cost to save them? What if an adequate presentation of the gospel was available to every Lezgi person? What if whole family units or even entire villages accepted His blessing, rather than to cling to the spiritual curses of their past? That is what we desperately pray for.

Fast and Pray for Many

In addition to daily personal abiding, we commit to extra seasons of prayer and fasting for mass movements of the unreached world to come to Jesus. We will pray and fast for the deep-seated demonic strongholds of the Silk Road to fall. We will pray that communities of faith in Jesus will grow sturdy roots to weather persecution as well as gain broad influence within their people group. We long to see people come to Christ the way they did on the day of Pentecost in Acts.

PRAY that missionaries will develop the spiritual depth to fast and pray in the way the early church did, so that there will be breakthroughs like those seen in the book of Acts.

PRAY that the few Lezgi believers will grow in perseverance as they introduce Jesus to their families and communities.

PRAY that Jesus would be found as the answer to the 658,000 Lezgi around the globe, about 193,000 of which make their home in Azerbaijan.

SENDING OUT (read by host)

YOU ARE THE

salt of the Earth

YOU ARE THE

light of the world.

As you go, glorify God.

(BASED ON MATTHEW 5:13-14)

INVITING IN (recite together)

Lord, you are our refuge,
our strength, and our help.

TEACH US TO STOP STRIVING,

To be still & know
That you are God.

You will be exalted
AMONG THE NATIONS;
You will be exalted
IN THE EARTH.

(BASED ON PSALMS 46:1, 10)

INWARD PRAYER (10 minutes)

Read individually

> Search me, God, and know my heart; test me and know my anxious thoughts. See if there is any offensive way in me, and lead me in the way everlasting. (Psalms 139:23, 24).

Silence

Confession & Accountability

How am I? What struggles am I facing today?

What is God's truth in the midst of this struggle?

Is there anything in my life that is creating a barrier between me and God or between me and a person in my life? If so, what should I do about it?

Reflect on God's forgiveness. Thank God for the help He is ready to give.

WORSHIP (15 minutes)

Sing together

Communion

WORD (10 minutes)

Read out loud together

    BIBLE STUDY: A church planter's farewell (Acts 20:13–38)

RESPONSE (25 minutes)

Respond to the Word as a group

What is God building IN our community through this Scripture?

    • *What is the main point of this passage?*

    • *How is this passage relevant to building communities of faith?*

- *What is the Lord teaching us through this passage?*

How can we mature as the body of Christ by living this OUT?

- *What elements of our church/small group's culture need growth/maturity?*

- *What part do each of us have to play to see the answer to the question above realized?*

- *How and when will we take action steps to do this?*

- *How will we keep each other accountable?*

How will we invest in those AROUND us to see more communities of faith in Jesus formed?

- *How will living this out help our community of faith better reflect Jesus to those around us?*

- *Who can we invite to discover Jesus with us?*

- *How will we actively work toward more communities of faith being formed?*

OUTWARD PRAYER (30 minutes)

Pray for each other

Pray for the people with whom you'll share

Pray for the Silk Road UPG on the following page

Kazakh

Kazakhs were once nomadic shepherds and their traditional meal includes a lamb's head, cooked and carved up. After the meal, a cross is carved into the forehead of the lamb. The meaning has been lost to these beautiful people but provides an amazing open door to sharing Jesus, the Good Shepherd.

For a few years, before running into visa problems, we were privileged to be involved in ministry geared toward reaching university students in Kazakhstan. Our final gathering with those students took place over a warm, spring weekend in Kazakhstan's largest city, Almaty. Multiple UPGs were represented that day, though primarily Kazakhs.

Over the course of the weekend retreat, I shared four messages: "Who Is God," "Who Is Jesus," "Who Is the Holy Spirit," and "Who Is the Church." Up until that gathering, none of those students had ever been challenged to think about those questions. Every time I think about that weekend, I am reminded of the truth right before the eyes of the Kazakhs, yet they lack people to tell them the answers to these basic questions. They lack people to remind them of the heritage of the lamb and the cross within their own culture. Jesus is the Lamb of God, crucified for them. He is God with us. He is the Shepherd who seeks to save the lost.

Equip and Encourage

We commit to intentionally work together to be equipped to do the work of church planting. In doing so, we place a high priority on language learning, cultural acquisition, and missiological training. Against our naturally selfish and proud inclinations, we will strive to not compare our abilities and achievements with our teammates and colleagues, but rather rejoice in each other's success. We understand that these are a means to an end, not the goal itself; mere scaffolding that helps up build the church.

PRAY that missionaries will lay down a spirit of judgment and comparison to cheer one another on in ministry competency as they keep their eyes on the ultimate goal.

PRAY that the small communities of faith in Jesus found in Kazakhstan will be Spirit-led as they try to balance cultural relevance and faithfulness to the gospel.

PRAY for the roughly 14,400,000 Kazakh in Kazakhstan and its neighboring countries who need to hear a culturally relevant presentation of the good news.

SENDING OUT (read by host)

YOU ARE THE

salt of the Earth

YOU ARE THE

light of the world.

As you go, glorify God.

(BASED ON MATTHEW 5:13-14)

INVITING IN (recite together)

Lord, you are our refuge,
our strength, and our help.

TEACH US TO STOP STRIVING,

To be still & know
That you are God.

You will be exalted
AMONG THE NATIONS;

You will be exalted
IN THE EARTH.

(BASED ON PSALMS 46:1, 10)

INWARD PRAYER (10 minutes)

Read individually

> Search me, God, and know my heart; test me and know my anxious thoughts. See if there is any offensive way in me, and lead me in the way everlasting. (Psalms 139:23, 24).

Silence

Confession & Accountability

How am I? What struggles am I facing today?

What is God's truth in the midst of this struggle?

Is there anything in my life that is creating a barrier between me and God or between me and a person in my life? If so, what should I do about it?

Reflect on God's forgiveness. Thank God for the help He is ready to give.

WORSHIP (15 minutes)

Sing together

Communion

WORD (10 minutes)

Read out loud together

    BIBLE STUDY: A letter to brothers and sisters in Christ (Eph. 1:1–2:10)

RESPONSE (25 minutes)

Respond to the Word as a group

What is God building IN our community through this Scripture?

    • *What is the main point of this passage?*

    • *How is this passage relevant to building communities of faith?*

- *What is the Lord teaching us through this passage?*

How can we mature as the body of Christ by living this OUT?

- *What elements of our church/small group's culture need growth/maturity?*

- *What part do each of us have to play to see the answer to the question above realized?*

- *How and when will we take action steps to do this?*

- *How will we keep each other accountable?*

How will we invest in those AROUND us to see more communities of faith in Jesus formed?

- *How will living this out help our community of faith better reflect Jesus to those around us?*

- *Who can we invite to discover Jesus with us?*

- *How will we actively work toward more communities of faith being formed?*

OUTWARD PRAYER (30 minutes)

Pray for each other

Pray for the people with whom you'll share

Pray for the Silk Road UPG on the following page

Photo source: Joshua Project (joshuaproject.net)

UNREACHED PEOPLE GROUP: Yara[4]

Copious amounts of food, the house crowded with family and friends, games, and lots of laughter. Big Thanksgiving celebrations have always been a tradition in our family, and moving to the Silk Road provided no cause for a break in the tradition. The difference this particular year was that there were four distinct languages being spoken by the dozens of people crammed into our dining room. Among them was a young Yara family, and we were eager to see their reaction to the testimonies that would be shared that evening. As the plates were cleared, we began to share, one after another, the things for which we were thankful. Many in the room shared how thankful they were to know Jesus as God and to be free of their sins. I smiled through the tears as new believers and old saints alike spoke about the goodness of God. Many of our Muslim friends did not share, but the husband of the Yara family spoke up. He told us of his new faith, and how he loved Jesus now.

We shared a final prayer and several families left, while others stayed for hours more to play charades. The young Yara wife smiled through the whole evening. She was the most enthusiastic of all the charade players and thanked us profusely as she left. "I've never had fun like this," she said, "and I've never in my life heard such wonderful stories." Weeks later a friend of ours drove this wonderful lady to a doctor's appointment. When she asked her what she thought of that evening, she simply said, "Now we are true sisters because I have decided to follow Jesus as well."

[4]The Yara is one example of UPG populations which are extremely small and losing distinct ethnolinguistic markers as they assimilate into the larger people groups that surround them. For security purposes due to an increase of persecution among this small people group, a pseudonym has been used. Yara portrait based on photo from Joshua Project (joshuaproject.net).

Sow Broadly

Just as the farmer scatters seed everywhere, in Jesus' parable of the sower (Matt. 13:1-23), we commit to share the good news of Jesus as broadly as possible—with neighbors, friends, shopkeepers, strangers—with everyone. We will verbalize the gospel often, without allowing fear, prejudice, or apathy to hinder our proclamation.

PRAY that missionaries will be persistent in the constant and bold proclamation of the message of Jesus to as many people as possible, driven by the words of Romans 10:14, "…how can they believe in the one of whom they have not heard? And how can they hear without someone preaching to them?"

PRAY that the few Yara believers—as local and linguistic insiders—will have the confidence to share the simple and sweet message of the cross with family, friends, neighbors, and strangers without being held back by the fear of inevitable persecution.

PRAY that the estimated 3,000–5,000 Yara found only in portions of the Silk Road region will have access to the gospel message in their heart language.

SENDING OUT (read by host)

YOU ARE THE

salt of the Earth

YOU ARE THE

light of the world.

As you go, glorify God.

(BASED ON MATTHEW 5:13-14)

INVITING IN (recite together)

Lord, you are our refuge,
our strength, and our help.

TEACH US TO STOP STRIVING,

To be still & know
That you are God.

You will be exalted
AMONG THE NATIONS;
You will be exalted
IN THE EARTH.

(BASED ON PSALMS 46:1, 10)

INWARD PRAYER (10 minutes)

Read individually

> Search me, God, and know my heart; test me and know my anxious thoughts. See if there is any offensive way in me, and lead me in the way everlasting. (Psalms 139:23, 24).

Silence

Confession & Accountability

How am I? What struggles am I facing today?

What is God's truth in the midst of this struggle?

Is there anything in my life that is creating a barrier between me and God or between me and a person in my life? If so, what should I do about it?

Reflect on God's forgiveness. Thank God for the help He is ready to give.

WORSHIP (15 minutes)

Sing together

Communion

WORD (10 minutes)

Read out loud together

BIBLE STUDY: Walls of division broken down (Eph. 2:11–3:21)

RESPONSE (25 minutes)

Respond to the Word as a group

What is God building IN our community through this Scripture?

- *What is the main point of this passage?*

- *How is this passage relevant to building communities of faith?*

- *What is the Lord teaching us through this passage?*

How can we mature as the body of Christ by living this OUT?

- *What elements of our church/small group's culture need growth/maturity?*

- *What part do each of us have to play to see the answer to the question above realized?*

- *How and when will we take action steps to do this?*

- *How will we keep each other accountable?*

How will we invest in those AROUND us to see more communities of faith in Jesus formed?

- *How will living this out help our community of faith better reflect Jesus to those around us?*

- *Who can we invite to discover Jesus with us?*

- *How will we actively work toward more communities of faith being formed?*

OUTWARD PRAYER (30 minutes)

Pray for each other

Pray for the people with whom you'll share

Pray for the Silk Road UPG on the following page

UNREACHED
PEOPLE
GROUP:

Dungan

The phone rang early one morning: "You must come to my home. Your husband must be here at 10 and you at 2." Our English student and dear friend Farishta, a Dungan woman, wanted us to attend the meal marking the fortieth day after her mother-in-law had passed away. As in most Muslim cultures along the Silk Road, a feast accompanying the reading of the Koran is hosted at various intervals after the death of a loved one.

My husband arrived to a packed house. He was seated on the floor with the village elders and religious leaders. Sitting across from him was the imam from the nearby mosque. They had conversation over traditional foods, and after that, came the time for saying *namaz*, the Muslim ritual prayers.

That afternoon was my turn. The women gathered to eat the leftovers of the morning feast: rice mixed with meat, garlic, carrots, onion, and plenty of oil. We ate and talked, and after a while an elderly woman who was the local shaman came to the house. She sat on the floor in the room next to me, surrounded by candles. I understood very little of what she said, but I could feel the dark spiritual atmosphere around her. She led the women in prayers, but these prayers were to the spirits rather than to Allah. It was so apparent that day, as it is for many people groups along the Silk Road, that Islam is only a veneer over ancient and demonic tribal religions. These spiritual chains bind unreached peoples, generation by generation, but Jesus can bring freedom.

Sow Intentionally

As we sow broadly, we also commit to sow intentionally. We will endeavor to learn where people go when they are spiritually hungry and go there. We will encourage hearers of the Word to be sharers of the Word from the beginning, regardless of whether they have made a confession of faith or not. We will not just reach out to disenfranchised individuals but invite families and groups of friends to discover God through the Holy Scripture. We will pray that those who are passionate for and influential in their communities will come to Jesus.

PRAY that missionaries will have discernment in spiritually charged situations, protection from the attacks of the enemy, and wisdom in discipling communities to faith.

PRAY for the Word of God and the Spirit of truth to rise among the Dungan for an indigenous movement of faith in Christ.

PRAY for the nearly 118,000 Dungan around the globe, about 66,000 of which make their home in Kyrgyzstan.

SENDING OUT (read by host)

YOU ARE THE

salt of the Earth

YOU ARE THE

light of the world.

As you go, glorify God.

(BASED ON MATTHEW 5:13-14)

INVITING IN (recite together)

Lord, you are our refuge,
our strength, and our help.

TEACH US TO STOP STRIVING,

To be still & know
That you are God.

You will be exalted
AMONG THE NATIONS;
You will be exalted
IN THE EARTH.

(BASED ON PSALMS 46:1, 10)

INWARD PRAYER (10 minutes)

Read individually

> Search me, God, and know my heart; test me and know my anxious thoughts. See if there is any offensive way in me, and lead me in the way everlasting. (Psalms 139:23, 24).

Silence

Confession & Accountability

How am I? What struggles am I facing today?

What is God's truth in the midst of this struggle?

Is there anything in my life that is creating a barrier between me and God or between me and a person in my life? If so, what should I do about it?

Reflect on God's forgiveness. Thank God for the help He is ready to give.

WORSHIP (15 minutes)

Sing together

Communion

WORD (10 minutes)

Read out loud together

> **BIBLE STUDY:** Lives defined by quiet holiness, rather than meaningless talk (1 Tim. 1:1–2:15)

RESPONSE (25 minutes)

Respond to the Word as a group

What is God building IN our community through this Scripture?

- *What is the main point of this passage?*

- *How is this passage relevant to building communities of faith?*

- *What is the Lord teaching us through this passage?*

How can we mature as the body of Christ by living this OUT?

- *What elements of our church/small group's culture need growth/maturity?*

- *What part do each of us have to play to see the answer to the question above realized?*

- *How and when will we take action steps to do this?*

- *How will we keep each other accountable?*

How will we invest in those AROUND us to see more communities of faith in Jesus formed?

- *How will living this out help our community of faith better reflect Jesus to those around us?*

- *Who can we invite to discover Jesus with us?*

- *How will we actively work toward more communities of faith being formed?*

OUTWARD PRAYER (30 minutes)

Pray for each other

Pray for the people with whom you'll share

Pray for the Silk Road UPG on the following page

UNREACHED PEOPLE GROUP: Kashmiri

Hamid walked into the room filled with people. A young woman lay unconscious on a bed. She was restrained by a sheet wrapped around her. For years Rani had been tormented by demons, but for the past four days, she had been uncontrollable as demons manifested in and through her body. Her father was a respected imam in his city, and he was desperate for the deliverance of his daughter. They tried everything they knew—doctors, "holy men," and spiritists—yet no medicine, incantation, or amulet brought any relief. In fact, they only made her worse.

Suddenly, all eyes were on this teenage boy who recently came to know Isa al Mesih, Jesus the Messiah, as his Savior. I was privileged to be discipling this young man, and we had seen Isa do some amazing miracles in Hamid's family. He knew of the healing power in Jesus' name. He placed his hand on Rani's head and prayed, "Oh, Lord, You are Jesus! Our faith is in You! Your Word says that the power for healing of all kinds of diseases, 'I AM'! So I ask You, in the name of Jesus the Messiah, to heal her. Amen."

A peace came over Rani. She had a vision of a man in white who reached out and touched her. He said, "I am Isa al Mesih. I will heal you and set you free. I am always with you." Immediately, the demon left her. The family began to ask many questions. Over the next few weeks, they received a copy of the Injil. Rani's father quit his post as imam and eventually stopped going to the mosque all together. Jesus the Messiah had entered their world and brought the light of salvation into a spiritually dark region. It's only the beginning for the Kashmiri people group!

Invite God's Intervention

We commit to believe for miracles, healing, and open hearts as we go about the business of sharing the good news of Jesus. We will pray that God leads us to those who are ready to listen and receive the good news. We will pray for the revelation of Jesus through dreams and visions. Respectfully and lovingly, but without fear of being socially awkward, we will offer to pray for people on the spot as we understand their needs for God's intervention in their bodies, spirits, and social circumstances.

PRAY that missionaries will be prepared to fight this spiritual battle with spiritual weapons, relying on God's intervention rather than their own wit or strength.

PRAY that the minor number of Kashmiri believers will make a major impact on their people and nation through bold prayer and an unwavering commitment to Jesus.

PRAY for the 8,000,000 Kashmiri people, over 1,000,000 of which are in Pakistan and the remaining number in India, who desperately need God's intervention.

SENDING OUT (read by host)

YOU ARE THE

salt of the Earth

YOU ARE THE

light of the world.

As you go, glorify God.

(BASED ON MATTHEW 5:13-14)

INVITING IN (recite together)

Lord, you are our refuge,
our strength, and our help.

TEACH US TO STOP STRIVING,

To be still & know
That you are God.

You will be exalted

AMONG THE NATIONS;

You will be exalted

IN THE EARTH.

(BASED ON PSALMS 46:1, 10)

INWARD PRAYER (10 minutes)

Read individually

> Search me, God, and know my heart; test me and know my anxious thoughts. See if there is any offensive way in me, and lead me in the way everlasting. (Psalms 139:23, 24).

Silence

Confession & Accountability

How am I? What struggles am I facing today?

What is God's truth in the midst of this struggle?

Is there anything in my life that is creating a barrier between me and God or between me and a person in my life? If so, what should I do about it?

Reflect on God's forgiveness. Thank God for the help He is ready to give.

WORSHIP (15 minutes)

Sing together

Communion

WORD (10 minutes)

Read out loud together

> **BIBLE STUDY:** Those equipped for serving the church (Eph. 4:1–16; 1 Tim. 3:1–16)

RESPONSE (25 minutes)

Respond to the Word as a group

What is God building IN our community through these Scriptures?

- *What is the main point of these passages?*

- *How are these passages relevant to building communities of faith?*

- *What is the Lord teaching us through these passages?*

How can we mature as the body of Christ by living this OUT?

- *What elements of our church/small group's culture need growth/maturity?*

- *What part do each of us have to play to see the answer to the question above realized?*

- *How and when will we take action steps to do this?*

- *How will we keep each other accountable?*

How will we invest in those AROUND us to see more communities of faith in Jesus formed?

- *How will living this out help our community of faith better reflect Jesus to those around us?*

- *Who can we invite to discover Jesus with us?*

- *How will we actively work toward more communities of faith being formed?*

OUTWARD PRAYER (30 minutes)

Pray for each other

Pray for the people with whom you'll share

Pray for the Silk Road UPG on the following page

UNREACHED PEOPLE GROUPS: *Muslim Refugee Communities*

One afternoon we stopped for lunch at a small Syrian restaurant on a busy Turkish street. *"Ahlan wa sahlan!"* the man at the door warmly welcomed in his native Arabic tongue as he motioned for us to have a seat. Behind the tin façade hiding the kitchen, a perspiring cook prepared our order of falafel and shawarma sandwiches. The un-level table rocked back and forth every time we shifted our weight. Nothing but a clock and a calendar with Arabic calligraphy decorated the worn walls.

As we waited we talked with the restaurant's owner, Omar, getting to know his story. Back in his hometown in Syria, he had been the owner of four successful businesses. Then one day, ISIS came to his city and killed several people next door and burned one of his businesses to the ground. He decided then he had no other choice but to flee with his wife and children and leave behind the life they had always known and loved. Now in Turkey, he was able to open this modest sandwich shop and provide for his family. He acknowledged that they were fortunate compared to many of the refugees living on the streets and in makeshift shelters trying to survive. And yet, we could see that he still felt discouraged and hopeless.

The next time we stopped by Omar's restaurant it happened to be the day before Easter. Omar was excited to see us and we were soon engaged in conversation. As we talked, he brought up the subject of our faiths, asking me what was different about what we believed. This was an open door to share with him what we as Jesus-followers would be celebrating the very next day. He listened, intrigued with what I had to say. It was most likely the first time he ever heard the basic message of the gospel. How desperately we want him to encounter the God who beckons us to come to Him with our burdens and find abundant life and the peace that transcends our circumstances.

Like Omar, millions of Syrians—along with people from Afghanistan, Iraq, Iran, Somalia and other regions of North Africa, the Middle East, and the Silk Road—have been faced with the decision to either sustain a broken existence, displaced in their own war-torn and otherwise hostile home countries, or flee to neighboring countries in hope of finding protection and the pursuit of a new life. Our world is now experiencing one of the worst humanitarian crises, replete with complexities, flanked with sorrow.

Although Live Dead Silk Road's church planting initiatives focus on the UPGs of a specific nine-country region of Central Eurasia, we recognize that the refugee crisis has brought a broad array of unreached, unengaged Muslim people groups to us. While we do not concentrate on compassion work, as many other great ministries exist to do, we want our spiritual eyes to be perceptive to the opportunity to plant the seed of the gospel among everyone, especially those who have come out of an environment where there is no chance of encountering the gospel

Articulate The Gospel

We commit to boldly and unashamedly articulate the gospel—the good news of Jesus, which is the power of God for salvation to everyone who believes (Rom. 1:16). We will identify ourselves as Christ-followers early on in conversation and be aware of opportunities to direct our conversation to the gospel. We will not be content with only sharing spiritual suggestions or nuggets of truth. While making friendly conversation, being a good person, and even sharing a testimony is important for witness, all falls short if we have not fluently and appropriately proclaimed the core of salvation though Jesus.

PRAY that missionaries will vigilantly prepare for moments like this—not just to offer spiritual suggestions, but to boldly and fluently share the core of salvation through Jesus.

PRAY that believers from a Muslim background will catch the vision of sharing Jesus with and planting the church among those who are unreached and unengaged with the gospel at all costs.

PRAY for the staggering millions of refugees and forcibly displaced peoples flooding the Silk Road and the rest of the world. Pray especially that Muslim refugees will have a chance that they likely would not have had in their home countries—to hear the good news.

SENDING OUT (read by host)

YOU ARE THE

salt of the Earth

YOU ARE THE

light of the world.

As you go, glorify God.

(BASED ON MATTHEW 5:13-14)

INVITING IN (recite together)

Lord, you are our refuge,
our strength, and our help.

TEACH US TO STOP STRIVING,

To be still & know That you are God.

You will be exalted

AMONG THE NATIONS;

You will be exalted

IN THE EARTH.

(BASED ON PSALMS 46:1, 10)

INWARD PRAYER (10 minutes)

Read individually

> Search me, God, and know my heart; test me and know my anxious thoughts. See if there is any offensive way in me, and lead me in the way everlasting. (Psalms 139:23, 24).

Silence

Confession & Accountability

How am I? What struggles am I facing today?

What is God's truth in the midst of this struggle?

Is there anything in my life that is creating a barrier between me and God or between me and a person in my life? If so, what should I do about it?

Reflect on God's forgiveness. Thank God for the help He is ready to give.

WORSHIP (15 minutes)

Sing together

Communion

WORD (10 minutes)

Read out loud together

> **BIBLE STUDY:** Lead by example (Eph. 4:17–5:20; 1 Tim. 4:1–16)

RESPONSE (25 minutes)

Respond to the Word as a group

What is God building IN our community through these Scriptures?

- *What is the main point of these passages?*

- *How are these passages relevant to building communities of faith?*

- *What is the Lord teaching us through these passages?*

How can we mature as the body of Christ by living this OUT?

- *What elements of our church/small group's culture need growth/maturity?*

- *What part do each of us have to play to see the answer to the question above realized?*

- *How and when will we take action steps to do this?*

- *How will we keep each other accountable?*

How will we invest in those AROUND us to see more communities of faith in Jesus formed?

- *How will living this out help our community of faith better reflect Jesus to those around us?*

- *Who can we invite to discover Jesus with us?*

- *How will we actively work toward more communities of faith being formed?*

OUTWARD PRAYER (30 minutes)

Pray for each other

Pray for the people with whom you'll share

Pray for the Silk Road UPG on the following page

UNREACHED PEOPLE GROUP: Turkmen

Turkmenistan is a country notorious for its lack of connection to the outside world and its attempts to shield its people from information. This includes information about religion, even Islam, the predominant religion of Turkmenistan.

The effects of this government repression were evident one night when we had a Turkmen girl, Gul, in our home for dinner and conversation. Gul was a regular guest in our home, and she came, often after the children were in bed, and sat for hours with us on the floor where we shared meals together (usually chicken, as that was her favorite). Even though she was in a foreign country studying international business and had studied English for a year, she was surprised to learn from us that the United States and England were not only not physically connected to one another but were separate countries altogether. When the topic turned to religion and Isa Mesih ("Jesus Christ" in the Turkmen language), she was certain that the word "Mesih" must not be Turkmen as she had never heard it before. Considering that Islam accepts the title "Mesih" for Jesus yet treats Him only as a prophet, the fact that she had never heard the word before was even more incredible.

While government oppression ensures the people of Turkmenistan remain only loosely connected to their own religion, it also shields them from hearing or knowing anything about the only One that can save them.

Invite a Response to the Gospel

Rather than relegating conversations about Jesus to an interesting exchange of religious ideas, we commit to gently but boldly encourage hearers of the gospel to respond. Some will reject Jesus, others will be vague, and some will express readiness to begin a journey of discovery of God's Word. By inviting a response to the gospel, we will have a better filter for how to follow-up with them.

PRAY that missionaries will not be hesitant in inviting—even challenging— people to respond to the gospel, and for discernment in how to follow-up.

PRAY for solid teaching and courage for the few Turkmen who have heard and responded to the good news of Jesus.

PRAY for the over 8,000,000 Turkmen scattered throughout Turkmenistan, its neighboring countries, and abroad, who have been utterly sheltered from news of the gospel.

SENDING OUT (read by host)

YOU ARE THE

salt of the Earth

YOU ARE THE

light of the world.

As you go, glorify God.

(BASED ON MATTHEW 5:13-14)

*Lord, you are our refuge,
our strength, and our help.*

TEACH US TO STOP STRIVING,

To be still & know
That you are God.

You will be exalted
AMONG THE NATIONS;
You will be exalted
IN THE EARTH.

(BASED ON PSALMS 46:1, 10)

INWARD PRAYER (10 minutes)

Read individually

> Search me, God, and know my heart; test me and know my anxious thoughts. See if there is any offensive way in me, and lead me in the way everlasting. (Psalms 139:23, 24).

Silence

Confession & Accountability

How am I? What struggles am I facing today?

What is God's truth in the midst of this struggle?

Is there anything in my life that is creating a barrier between me and God or between me and a person in my life? If so, what should I do about it?

Reflect on God's forgiveness. Thank God for the help He is ready to give.

WORSHIP (15 minutes)

Sing together

Communion

WORD (10 minutes)

Read out loud together

> **BIBLE STUDY:** Interpersonal relationships (Eph. 5:21–6:9;
> 1 Tim. 5:1–6:2)

RESPONSE (25 minutes)

Respond to the Word as a group

What is God building IN our community through these Scriptures?

- *What is the main point of these passages?*

- *How are these passages relevant to building communities of faith?*

- *What is the Lord teaching us through these passages?*

How can we mature as the body of Christ by living this OUT?

- *What elements of our church/small group's culture need growth/maturity?*

- *What part do each of us have to play to see the answer to the question above realized?*

- *How and when will we take action steps to do this?*

- *How will we keep each other accountable?*

How will we invest in those AROUND us to see more communities of faith in Jesus formed?

- *How will living this out help our community of faith better reflect Jesus to those around us?*

- *Who can we invite to discover Jesus with us?*

- *How will we actively work toward more communities of faith being formed?*

OUTWARD PRAYER (30 minutes)

Pray for each other

Pray for the people with whom you'll share

Pray for the Silk Road UPG on the following page

UNREACHED
PEOPLE
GROUP: *Kurds*

A teammate and I were walking the streets, praying and looking for an opportunity to share Jesus. We stepped into a tiny store to buy water. A petite, unassuming woman with a quiet smile offered us tea and after introductions and small talk, she shared that her husband was dying of cancer. They moved from their remote village among the dusty rolling hills of southern Turkey's Syrian border to the cosmopolitan metropolis of Istanbul for medical treatment. We prayed for healing in Jesus' name and promised to visit again.

We returned soon only to find the shop closed down, but a few weeks later as we happened to pass by on the bus, we were surprised to see it open again. Returning, we found the husband whom we prayed for just a few weeks earlier. Together the couple introduced us to their children and invited us to their home for dinner. Upon entering their basement apartment, we met more family members including the husband's stern-faced father and his mother who was dressed all in white which had a camouflage effect against the lace window coverings. As dinner time approached we were seated around a blue-and-white checkered tablecloth spread on the living room floor surrounded by welcoming faces. They treated us as family. We ate from small clay pots filled with steamy vegetables, complimented by salad and bowls filled with a deep red-colored stew and tiny glasses frothing with a freshly made yogurt drink.

It was in this setting, a large family gathered with wide eyes and eager ears, that we shared stories of Jesus' power and Lordship and prayed for healing in His name. They sat in awe and wonder as we shared the truth about Jesus. There are so many Kurdish families just like them who have not had access to the truth of Jesus, and will not until someone comes and shares a cup of tea or a meal and starts to tell a story.

Follow-up Immediately

We commit to follow-up immediately with those who have responded positively to the gospel. We will not be so attached to our agenda that we miss an opportunity to lead a person or community of people to Jesus and begin to teach them what it means to follow Him. Our families and teams will understand and support the necessity of dropping everything for a time for the sake of investing in those who are ready to accept the good news.

PRAY that missionaries will have the discernment and willingness to abandon what keeps them merely busy and invest in what will move forward God's vision for the church among the unreached.

PRAY that Kurdish believers will be a bold, strong voice for the hope that Jesus offers.

PRAY for the roughly 15,000,000 Kurds around the globe, mostly found in Turkey and its neighboring countries, who urgently need the peace of God.

SENDING OUT (read by host)

YOU ARE THE

salt of the Earth

YOU ARE THE

light of the world.

As you go, glorify God.

(BASED ON MATTHEW 5:13-14)

INVITING IN (recite together)

Lord, you are our refuge,
our strength, and our help.

TEACH US TO STOP STRIVING,

To be still & know that you are God.

You will be exalted

AMONG THE NATIONS;

You will be exalted

IN THE EARTH.

(BASED ON PSALMS 46:1, 10)

INWARD PRAYER (10 minutes)

Read individually

> Search me, God, and know my heart; test me and know my anxious thoughts. See if there is any offensive way in me, and lead me in the way everlasting. (Psalms 139:23, 24).

Silence

Confession & Accountability

How am I? What struggles am I facing today?

What is God's truth in the midst of this struggle?

Is there anything in my life that is creating a barrier between me and God or between me and a person in my life? If so, what should I do about it?

Reflect on God's forgiveness. Thank God for the help He is ready to give.

WORSHIP (15 minutes)

Sing together

Communion

WORD (10 minutes)

Read out loud together

> **BIBLE STUDY:** Fight the good fight of faith (Eph. 6:10–24; 1 Tim. 6:3–21)

RESPONSE (25 minutes)

Respond to the Word as a group

What is God building IN our community through these Scriptures?

- *What is the main point of these passages?*

- *How are these passages relevant to building communities of faith?*

- *What is the Lord teaching us through these passages?*

How can we mature as the body of Christ by living this OUT?

- *What elements of our church/small group's culture need growth/maturity?*

- *What part do each of us have to play to see the answer to the question above realized?*

- *How and when will we take action steps to do this?*

- *How will we keep each other accountable?*

How will we invest in those AROUND us to see more communities of faith in Jesus formed?

- *How will living this out help our community of faith better reflect Jesus to those around us?*

- *Who can we invite to discover Jesus with us?*

- *How will we actively work toward more communities of faith being formed?*

OUTWARD PRAYER (30 minutes)

Pray for each other

Pray for the people with whom you'll share

Pray for the Silk Road UPG on the following page

UNREACHED
PEOPLE
GROUP: Tatar

G uzal was a bit cold and stand-offish toward us at first, simply executing her job
as a lawyer when we came in need of some legal services. But as we worked
together more and as we started inviting her into our home for tea, she warmed up.
We shared the gospel with her, and to our surprise she expressed that she, like us,
was a believer in Jesus! This was the first time we met a Tatar believer in the region
we lived.

Guzal confided that she was very fearful about telling other people she is a Christian, which perhaps explains her hesitancy to be open with us at first. She had found a local church to attend, which was a good distance from where she lived with her mother, but was not involved in any intentional discipleship. As our relationship with Guzal deepened, we began to meet together with her and her mother to read the Bible and pray. Through this process of discipleship, we saw Guzal's faith in Jesus deepen, and as a result her mother decided to commit her life to Christ as well.

Up until that point Guzal's mother had been very resistant to the gospel. Since Guzal's father had passed away, there was no man in the family to provide a covering for them or to help them with certain work around the house. Because of this, acceptance in their community was extremely important, and already those in the community who knew Guzal was a Christian treated her differently. As they walked through their village on the outskirts of the city, their neighbors refused to even greet them. Guzal's mother made the costly decision to put aside this obstacle as she put her faith in Jesus.

Although we had to move to a different country, we still have a good relationship with Guzal and her mother. It is a blessing to be a part of their journey in growing deeper as disciples of Jesus. We pray that many more Tatar will know and follow Him just like Guzal and her mother.

Cultivate Active Participation in the Faith

As Jesus teaches in the parable of the wise and foolish builders (Matt. 7:21-27), we commit to teach those on the journey of faith to not just be hearers, but to put His words into practice. We will help Jesus followers to not just gain knowledge but become active participants in the faith. We will model thinking and acting on the application of God's Word and being attentive to the guidance of the Holy Spirit. We will lovingly keep one another accountable to grow in obedience to Jesus.

PRAY that missionaries will be equipped in language, in spiritual maturity, and with practical discipleship tools as they disciple MBBs.

PRAY that local Christians will have the courage and spiritual depth to lead in modeling and encouraging active participation in the faith as they reach out to Tatar communities throughout the Silk Road.

PRAY for the approximately 6,400,000 Tatar around the globe, a great many of which live in Silk Road nations.

SENDING OUT (read by host)

YOU ARE THE

salt of the Earth

YOU ARE THE

light of the world.

As you go, glorify God.

(BASED ON MATTHEW 5:13-14)

INVITING IN (recite together)

*Lord, you are our refuge,
our strength, and our help.*

TEACH US TO STOP STRIVING,

To be still & know
That you are God.

You will be exalted

AMONG THE NATIONS;

You will be exalted

IN THE EARTH.

(BASED ON PSALMS 46:1, 10)

INWARD PRAYER (10 minutes)

Read individually

> Search me, God, and know my heart; test me and know my anxious thoughts. See if there is any offensive way in me, and lead me in the way everlasting. (Psalms 139:23, 24).

Silence

Confession & Accountability

How am I? What struggles am I facing today?

What is God's truth in the midst of this struggle?

Is there anything in my life that is creating a barrier between me and God or between me and a person in my life? If so, what should I do about it?

Reflect on God's forgiveness. Thank God for the help He is ready to give.

WORSHIP (15 minutes)

Sing together

Communion

WORD (10 minutes)

Read out loud together

    BIBLE STUDY: Be faithful to what was entrusted to you (2 Tim. 1:1–2:26)

RESPONSE (25 minutes)

Respond to the Word as a group

What is God building IN our community through this Scripture?

- *What is the main point of this passage?*

- *How is this passage relevant to building communities of faith?*

- *What is the Lord teaching us through these passages?*

How can we mature as the body of Christ by living this OUT?

- *What elements of our church/small group's culture need growth/maturity?*

- *What part do each of us have to play to see the answer to the question above realized?*

- *How and when will we take action steps to do this?*

- *How will we keep each other accountable?*

How will we invest in those AROUND us to see more communities of faith in Jesus formed?

- *How will living this out help our community of faith better reflect Jesus to those around us?*

- *Who can we invite to discover Jesus with us?*

- *How will we actively work toward more communities of faith being formed?*

OUTWARD PRAYER (30 minutes)

Pray for each other

Pray for the people with whom you'll share

Pray for the Silk Road UPG on the following page

UNREACHED
PEOPLE
GROUP: *Black Hat*[5]

In the dead of winter, a local pastor and a team of musicians set out on a 1,200-kilometer trip across rough roads to a city where they didn't know a single person. One night of their journey they slept in their frozen, broken-down van. They were able to fix it and eventually reach their destination.

The Lord put it in their hearts to plant a church amongst the people of the Black Hat, and they prayed for wisdom to know how to begin. The Lord gave them the idea of visiting people who were selling their houses, so their entire first day was spent looking at houses and sharing the gospel with the owners. Just as it grew dark and they wondered where they would sleep that night, they looked at a house whose owner gave her life to Jesus. She invited them to sleep there. That was the beginning of the church.

There was an incredible response, mainly among the young people. Sunday meetings quickly grew to about 500 people. The authorities were alarmed, but a local policeman testified how his own son's life had been changed by the Lord and how he was off drugs and drinking. The local pastor who first drove out there appointed three young Black Hat men, new believers, as pastors. He visited them regularly and sent other brothers to encourage them. To set a legal precedence, they tried to legally register "The Full Gospel Church of the People of the Black Hat." Registration, of course, was impossible. Nevertheless, the church grew, and churches started in other towns in the area. I had the privilege of attending a Christian wedding in the Black Hat region, and tears ran down my face as I listened to some elderly women in traditional dress sing "Jesus Is Lord" in their language. It wasn't long before the young church began to compose their own worship songs and make beautiful contextualized art reflecting stories of the Bible.

But then officials finally reacted. Police raided the apartments of the three young pastors. Drugs were found, so they said, and the young men were quickly tried and imprisoned for 25 years each for being drug dealers. Unhindered by their circumstances, the young pastors took the opportunity to share the gospel to the others in prison, and many decided to follow Jesus. I spoke to one of these pastors after his time in prison, and he glowed with joy, just like the apostles of the early church in the book of Acts. Eventually, they were given amnesty but still lived under the shadow of their drug-dealing conviction. In the end the pastors and their young families moved to other countries. The Lord raised up others to take their place, and these church leaders continue to work while navigating the challenges of poverty, temptation, court hearings, large fines, and other forms of constant opposition.

[5]For security purposes due to an increase of persecution among this people group, a pseudonym has been used.

Model Church Well

We commit to model what it means to be a Christian community of faith in a way that is simple, natural, and culturally relevant so that believers can "be church" even if we are forced to leave or led to go to another pioneering context. We will not use methods, tools, or technology that is overly complex or unavailable to the local followers of Jesus. We will not bog down the function and practice of church with elements that are culturally comfortable to us but not biblically essential.

PRAY that missionaries will be willing to shed culturally comfortable models of evangelism, discipleship, and church and instead do the hard work of discovering what truly meets the spiritual needs of the people they are reaching out to.

PRAY that pastors of Black Hat churches will grow in wisdom and patient endurance as they lead people in the faith.

PRAY for the nearly 800,000 Black Hat spread across the Silk Road who still remain unreached.

SENDING OUT (read by host)

YOU ARE THE
salt of the Earth
YOU ARE THE
light of the world.
As you go, glorify God.

(BASED ON MATTHEW 5:13-14)

INVITING IN (recite together)

Lord, you are our refuge,
our strength, and our help.

TEACH US TO STOP STRIVING,

To be still & know
That you are God.

You will be exalted

AMONG THE NATIONS;

You will be exalted

IN THE EARTH.

(BASED ON PSALMS 46:1, 10)

INWARD PRAYER (10 minutes)

Read individually

> Search me, God, and know my heart; test me and know my anxious thoughts. See if there is any offensive way in me, and lead me in the way everlasting. (Psalms 139:23, 24).

Silence

Confession & Accountability

How am I? What struggles am I facing today?

What is God's truth in the midst of this struggle?

Is there anything in my life that is creating a barrier between me and God or between me and a person in my life? If so, what should I do about it?

Reflect on God's forgiveness. Thank God for the help He is ready to give.

WORSHIP (15 minutes)

Sing together

Communion

WORD (10 minutes)

Read out loud together

> **BIBLE STUDY:** Preach, teach, and live the Word (2 Tim. 3:1–4:22)

RESPONSE (25 minutes)

Respond to the Word as a group

What is God building IN our community through this Scripture?

- *What is the main point of this passage?*

- *How is this passage relevant to building communities of faith?*

- *What is the Lord teaching us through this passage?*

How can we mature as the body of Christ by living this OUT?

- *What elements of our church/small group's culture need growth/maturity?*

- *What part do each of us have to play to see the answer to the question above realized?*

- *How and when will we take action steps to do this?*

- *How will we keep each other accountable?*

How will we invest in those AROUND us to see more communities of faith in Jesus formed?

- *How will living this out help our community of faith better reflect Jesus to those around us?*

- *Who can we invite to discover Jesus with us?*

- *How will we actively work toward more communities of faith being formed?*

OUTWARD PRAYER (30 minutes)

Pray for each other

Pray for the people with whom you'll share

Pray for the Silk Road UPG on the following page

UNREACHED
PEOPLE
GROUP: *Baloch*

Before being forced to leave Pakistan, and now from a distance, I work closely with Rasheed, the only Jesus-follower from the Baloch-Lashari people group that we know of. This is his story.

Browsing through the bookshelves of the secondhand book shop, something caught Rasheed's eye. He picked it up and studied the cover.

It was an Injil, a New Testament. It didn't look too scary. Growing up in a devout Muslim home, Rasheed was a fanatical follower of the prophet Muhammed. He had a deep disdain for Christians and devoted his life to study the Koran and to become an imam. His teachers at the madrasah had warned him over and over to never read or even touch a Bible! Yet somehow their constant warnings only sparked a curiosity. "What could be so bad about a book?" In his heart he decided that if he ever came across a Bible or portion of it, he would read it in secret.

Many nights Rasheed studied the Injil in his bedroom, comparing it to the Koran. The more he read about what Jesus said about Himself, the more impressed he was, and over time, Rasheed discovered that he had been following the wrong man! "Jesus was the true Savior, and He is the only One who can save our soul," he thought. He needed time to think it through. In Pakistan a radical Muslim that leaves Islam to follow Jesus will most likely pay with his life. After counting the cost, Rasheed prayed to Jesus, "Thank you for giving Your life for me on the cross to save me! Forgive me of all my sins." Immediately, he was overwhelmed with a supernatural peace and joy in his heart. He promised Jesus to follow Him for the rest of his life.

One morning as Rasheed slept, his father and uncles barged into his bedroom door armed with iron rods. They cursed him as they beat him with no mercy. They called him a *kafir*, a religious traitor. As he felt his bones crush with each blow, he closed his eyes and prepared to meet his new Savior. When he awoke, Rasheed found himself in a hospital. The pain was unbearable. His body was wrapped in bandages due to all the wounds and broken bones. After this his family tried to kill him one more time, but the Lord rescued him from their wrath. Rasheed escaped and fled to another city where he committed his life to follow Jesus. He continues to share the gospel with other Muslims, that they, too, may experience God's saving grace.

Be Patient and Gracious

We commit to being persistent in patience and generous in grace with believers and the newly forming church. We will ask God to let us see them through His eyes—not the sin-tainted mess that they are, but as the holy ones of God. While empowering them to be leaders in the community of faith and lighthouses among their people group, we will try to be knowledgeable and empathetic to their unique and tumultuous identity now as a minority in their society.

PRAY that missionaries will grasp the complexities that believers of a Muslim background face, speaking into their lives with delicacy and Spirit-led discernment, and with a willingness to share in their suffering.

PRAY that the faith of this one believer among the Baloch-Lashari will ripple into communities of faith among all the Baloch tribes.

PRAY that the gospel will gain access to the estimated 15,000,000 Baloch people divided into over 130 tribes across Pakistan, Afghanistan, and Iraq despite the hostility of environment and vehement opposition to the Christian faith.

SENDING OUT (read by host)

YOU ARE THE
salt of the Earth
YOU ARE THE
light of the world.

As you go, glorify God.

(BASED ON MATTHEW 5:13-14)

INVITING IN (recite together)

Lord, you are our refuge,
our strength, and our help.

TEACH US TO STOP STRIVING,

To be still & know
That you are God.

You will be exalted
AMONG THE NATIONS;
You will be exalted
IN THE EARTH.

(BASED ON PSALMS 46:1, 10)

INWARD PRAYER (10 minutes)

Read individually

> Search me, God, and know my heart; test me and know my anxious thoughts. See if there is any offensive way in me, and lead me in the way everlasting. (Psalms 139:23, 24).

Silence

Confession & Accountability

How am I? What struggles am I facing today?

What is God's truth in the midst of this struggle?

Is there anything in my life that is creating a barrier between me and God or between me and a person in my life? If so, what should I do about it?

Reflect on God's forgiveness. Thank God for the help He is ready to give.

WORSHIP (15 minutes)

Sing together

Communion

WORD (10 minutes)

Read out loud together

> **BIBLE STUDY:** Jesus' message to the Ephesian church (Rev. 1:4–2:7)

RESPONSE (25 minutes)

Respond to the Word as a group

What is God building IN our community through this Scripture?

- *What is the main point of this passage?*

- *How is this passage relevant to building communities of faith?*

- *What is the Lord teaching us through this passage?*

How can we mature as the body of Christ by living this OUT?

- *What elements of our church/small group's culture need growth/maturity?*

- *What part do each of us have to play to see the answer to the question above realized?*

- *How and when will we take action steps to do this?*

- *How will we keep each other accountable?*

How will we invest in those AROUND us to see more communities of faith in Jesus formed?

- *How will living this out help our community of faith better reflect Jesus to those around us?*

- *Who can we invite to discover Jesus with us?*

- *How will we actively work toward more communities of faith being formed?*

OUTWARD PRAYER (30 minutes)

Pray for each other

Pray for the people with whom you'll share

Pray for the Silk Road UPG on the following page

UNENGAGED
UNREACHED
PEOPLE
GROUP: *Ingush*

There is no story for this people group. No one from our movement has had an experience with a person from this people group. Not only that, there is currently not a single known missionary from any organization involved in church planting among this people group. They are not only unreached, they are unengaged.

In the Silk Road, the places we find these people groups are called "Zero Zones," in other words, a region that has no known believers, likely no complete Bible translation or recording in this people group's heart language, no known churches, and no known missionaries living in and focusing on evangelism and church planting among the indigenous people of that region.

The data for unengaged unreached people groups (UUPGs) are dynamic, constantly changing with the ebb and flow of your prayerful awareness, missionary movement, obstacles that impede the work being done in some places, and the doors God supernaturally opens in others.

There is no guarantee that at the moment you read this, this people group remains in a Zero Zone, but what can be safely said is that many Zero Zones remain. Entire ethno-linguistic blocks may be still hidden from the radar or threaten too high a risk or for a myriad of other reasons continue to be unengaged. Pray for them all—the ones whose names you can't pronounce, the ones whose names you have yet to hear, the ones whom God is putting on your heart to reach out to with the beautiful message of Jesus.

"For, 'Everyone who calls on the name of the Lord will be saved.' How, then, can they call on the one they have not believed in? And how can they believe in the one of whom they have not heard? And how can they hear without someone preaching to them? And how can anyone preach unless they are sent? As it is written: 'How beautiful are the feet of those who bring good news!'" (Rom. 10:13–15).

Assess and Adapt

We commit to continually assess our role in the process of church planting and adapt appropriately. We will devote ourselves to facilitating the establishment of communities of believers, model obedience to Jesus, and empower Jesus followers to lead. As we do so, like Paul, we will keep our eyes open for the time to move on to the next place where the gospel is not being preached. We will not abandon the church while it is still in an infantile stage, nor will we stifle the health and maturity of the indigenous church by staying too long.

PRAY that missionaries will prayerfully assess when it is time to leave an established community of faith and have the discernment and courage to follow the Holy Spirit's leading to the next context where the gospel is not being preached.

PRAY that God puts a vision in the hearts of MBBs who neighbor these unengaged unreached people groups to boldly, lovingly, and wisely engage these communities with the gospel.

PRAY for the 21,000 Ingush spread across Kazakhstan, Kyrgyzstan, and Uzbekistan, plus over 400,000 Ingush in Russia, along with the estimated 3,207 unengaged unreached people groups, many of which are scattered throughout the Silk Road, who exist without an indigenous community of Jesus followers or a single boots-on-the-ground church planting team present to bring them the good news.

SENDING OUT (read by host)

YOU ARE THE

salt of the Earth

YOU ARE THE

light of the world.

As you go, glorify God.

(BASED ON MATTHEW 5:13-14)

EPILOGUE

The twelve walked along, arms loose at the sides of their bodies, gently bumping into each other, shoulder to shoulder, brusque heads of grain tickling their fingers, ears attentive to His voice. They had never felt so empowered, so excited, so intimidated by their future.

"The harvest is plentiful but the workers are few," Jesus said as His compassion-filled eyes looked over the crowds of people He had just been reaching out to. "Ask the Lord of the harvest, therefore, to send out workers into his harvest field."

As Jesus prepared them to go out, the realization that they were answering the exact prayer that they were praying was thrilling. And yet the fine print concerning the cost of self-sacrifice was not lost on them.

Jesus expressed these words before commissioning the twelve disciples (Matt. 9:37–38) and again as He sent out seventy more of His followers (Luke 10:2). As His followers today, isn't He saying the same thing to us? Pray for more workers… and go.

Are you ready to put your boots on the ground?

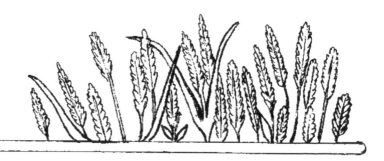

CONCLUSION

Thank you for abiding together over the course of these days and weeks. It has been a joy and privilege to put together this book, and we are truly thankful you have spent this time with us reflecting on God's Word in the context of the Silk Road and the UPGs we love.

Our hope in putting together this book was twofold: to provide a tool for abiding in Jesus with one another in fellowship, worship, prayer, study, reflection, and obedience, and to stimulate passionate prayer for UPGs and engagement with God's mission in the world today. I pray as you have worked through *Live Dead Together* that you have truly encountered the one true living God through His Son Jesus. As you meet with Him and draw closer to Him in community, I believe you will also find yourself drawn into the Lord's heart for the world—and particularly for those who have no access to the gospel today.

Now that you are done, you might be wondering: what next? We want you to stay engaged because we believe this book is just an introduction to the heart of God for our world. There are many ways to participate in God's mission among UPGs today. We would encourage you to check out the Live Dead website (www.livedead.org) for more information about starting a Live Dead Pray Band for a church planting team, participating financially in the work Live Dead does around the world, or finding your place by coming to join us where we live and work. Our teams have a variety of opportunities for followers of Jesus to put their time, energy, and skills to use in sharing the good news of Jesus the Messiah among those who have not heard.

MIDWEEK ABIDING: PART ONE

This section is designed to encourage and supplement abiding outside the group setting. The weekly reading for Part 1 is cohesive with the Scripture selections for the weekly group abiding and give the reader a chronological overview of the entire Bible in the course of twelve weeks.

Sin

Genesis 2:4–3:24 | Romans 3:9–24

Summary:
We all, like Adam and Eve, have turned away from God and in doing so have become estranged from Him.

Daily Reading:
1. Adam and Eve sin *(Gen. 2:4–3:24)*
2. Cain kills Abel *(Gen. 4:1–16)*
3. Noah saved from the flood *(Gen. 6:5–7:24)*
4. God's promise to Noah *(Gen. 8:1–9:17)*
5. God's covenant agreement with Abraham *(Gen. 12:1–9; 15:1–21)*
6. Ishmael and Isaac *(Gen. 16:1–17:23)*
7. Three visitors *(Gen. 18:1–15; 21:1–21)*

Memorize: *Romans 3:23–24*
For all have sinned and fall short of the glory of God, and all are justified freely by his grace through the redemption that came by Christ Jesus.

Sacrifice

Genesis 22:1–18 | Hebrews 9:19–10:10

Summary:
In the same way God provided a ram as a substitutional sacrifice in place of Abraham's son, God has provided the ultimate sacrifice to deliver us from eternal separation from Him.

Daily Reading:
1. A substitute for Abraham's son *(Gen. 22:1–18)*
2. Events in Jacob's life *(Gen. 25:19–34; 28:1–22)*
3. Moses' early years *(Exo. 1:1–2:25)*
4. God delivers His people *(Exo. 3:1–15; 12:21–42)*
5. Commands and sacrifices *(Exo. 20:1–17; Num. 28:1–25)*
6. Joshua leads to the Promised Land *(Josh. 1:1–9; 24:1–27)*
7. Israel's sin cycle and asking for a king *(Judges 2:7–19; 1 Sam. 12:6–13:14; 16:1–13)*

Memorize: *Hebrews 9:22*
In fact, the law requires that nearly everything be cleansed with blood, and without the shedding of blood there is no forgiveness.

Divine Forgiveness

2 Samuel 11:1–12:25 | Psalm 51 | 1 John 1:5–2:2

Summary:

Jesus is the prophesied Messiah, descended from King David. If we confess our sin and place our trust in His death and resurrection, God will forgive and restore us.

Daily Reading:

1. King David's sin and repentance *(2 Sam. 11:1–12:25; Psalm 51)*
2. A selection of King David's songs *(Psalms 19, 22, 23, 25, 103, 139)*
3. King Solomon *(1 Kings 2:1–3; 4:29–5:5; 11:1–13)*
4. Elijah challenges idolatry *(1 Kings 18:1–46)*
5. Exile and prophecies of judgment *(Eze. 14:12–23; Jer. 52:4–27; Lam. 3)*
6. Restoration *(Ezra 1:1–11; Neh. 8:13–9:38)*
7. The suffering servant *(Isa. 52:1–53:12)*

Memorize: *1 John 1:9*

If we confess our sins, he is faithful and just and will forgive us our sins and purify us from all unrighteousness.

Water Baptism

Luke 1:5–25, 57–80 | Luke 3:1–22 | Romans 6:1–11

Summary:

John the Baptist's call to repent and be baptized with water is a critical milestone in following Jesus.

Daily Reading:

1. John the Baptist's birth *(Luke 1:5–25, 57–80)*
2. Jesus' birth *(Luke 1:26–56; 2:1–20; Matt. 2:1–12)*
3. Jesus' circumcision and childhood *(Luke 2:21–52)*
4. Jesus' baptism *(Luke 3:1–22; John 1:19–34)*
5. Jesus tempted in the wilderness *(Luke 4:1–13)*
6. Jesus inaugurates His ministry *(Luke 4:14–44)*
7. Jesus' authority to forgive sins *(Luke 5:12–26)*

Memorize: *Romans 6:4*

We were therefore buried with him through baptism into death in order that, just as Christ was raised from the dead through the glory of the Father, we too may live a new life.

Following Jesus

Luke 5:1–11, 27–32 | John 15:1–17

Summary:
We have been given new life in Jesus and therefore should live accordingly to that new life. Jesus tells us that if we abide in Him, our lives will bear good fruit.

Daily Reading:
1. Jesus' call to follow Him *(Luke 5:1–11, 27–32)*
2. The woman at the well *(John 4:1–42)*
3. Jesus' sermon on the plain *(Luke 6:17–49)*
4. Jesus' criticism of religious legalism *(Matt. 5:17–42; Luke 11:37–54)*
5. Un-hypocritical prayer *(Matt. 6:1–18; Luke 11:5–13)*
6. Jesus' parables: The Good Samaritan and The Lost *(Luke 10:25–37; Luke 15:1–32)*
7. Kingdom of Heaven parables: The Sower, The Weeds, The Mustard Seed, The Yeast, The Treasure and Pearl *(Matt. 13:1–46)*

Memorize: *John 15:5*
I am the vine; you are the branches. If you remain in me and I in you, you will bear much fruit; apart from me you can do nothing.

Jesus' Authority

Luke 8:22–56 | John 14:1–14

Summary:

Jesus has all authority over the physical and spiritual world, and as His followers we pray in the authority of His name.

Daily Reading:

1. Jesus' authority over the spiritual and physical world *(Luke 8:22–56)*
2. More accounts of Jesus' authority *(Matt. 14:14–36)*
3. The Bread of Life *(John 6:25–71)*
4. The revelation of Jesus as Messiah to Peter *(Luke 9:18–36)*
5. Jesus' disciples sent out to minister *(Matt. 10:1–42; Luke 10:1–20)*
6. The resurrection of Lazarus and plot to kill Jesus *(John 11:1–57)*
7. Jesus enters Jerusalem *(Luke 19:28–20:19)*

Memorize: *John 14:12-13*

Very truly I tell you, whoever believes in me will do the works I have been doing, and they will do even greater things than these, because I am going to the Father. And I will do whatever you ask in my name, so that the Father may be glorified in the Son.

The Community of Faith

Luke 22:1–23 | Hebrews 10:19–25

Summary:
Meeting regularly with other followers of Jesus to encourage one another and remember His sacrificial death is a priority.

Daily Reading:

1. Jesus and His followers' last supper before the crucifixion *(Luke 22:1–23)*
2. Final instructions *(John 13:33–15:17)*
3. Betrayed, tried, and denied *(Matt. 26:36–75; John 18:28–40)*
4. Beaten and crucified *(John 19:1–37; Mark 15:27–39)*
5. Burial and resurrection *(Matt. 27:57–28:15; Luke 24:1–12, 36–49)*
6. Jesus' talk with Peter *(John 21:1–24)*
7. Last words and the ascension *(Matt. 28:16–20; Mark 16:15–20; Acts 1:3–11)*

Memorize: *Hebrews 10:24–25*
And let us consider how we may spur one another on toward love and good deeds, not giving up meeting together, as some are in the habit of doing, but encouraging one another—and all the more as you see the Day approaching.

The Holy Spirit

Acts 2:1–42 | John 14:15–27

Summary:
The Holy Spirit is Jesus' gift to those who follow Him, filling us with boldness to proclaim the gospel, reminding us of the truth of God's Word, and providing peace.

Daily Reading:
1. Jesus' followers baptized with the Holy Spirit *(Acts 2:1–42)*
2. Healing in Jesus' name *(Acts 3:1–26)*
3. Boldness despite opposition *(Acts 4:1–31)*
4. Ananias' and Sapphira's deception *(Acts 4:32–5:11)*
5. Obeying God rather than men *(Acts 5:12–42)*
6. Stephen, full of the Spirit and wisdom *(Acts 6:1–15)*
7. Stephen's sermon *(Acts 7:1–53)*

Memorize: *John 14:26*
But the Advocate, the Holy Spirit, whom the Father will send in my name, will teach you all things and will remind you of everything I have said to you.

Suffering

Acts 6:8–8:3 | Romans 8:1–39

Summary:

Embracing the good news of salvation through Jesus is worth the internal struggle of letting go of our own selfish desires and even suffering persecution from others.

Daily Reading:

1. The martyrdom of Stephen *(Acts 7:54–8:3)*
2. Saul's conversion *(Acts 9:1–31)*
3. Peter and Cornelius *(Acts 10:1–11:18)*
4. James executed but Peter delivered *(Acts 12:1–19)*
5. Barnabas and Saul sent out *(Acts 13:1–52)*
6. The Jerusalem Council *(Acts 15:1–35)*
7. Justified by faith *(Gal. 2:11–3:29)*

Memorize: *Romans 8:35–39*

Who shall separate us from the love of Christ? Shall trouble or hardship or persecution or famine or nakedness or danger or sword? As it is written: "For your sake we face death all day long; we are considered as sheep to be slaughtered."

No, in all these things we are more than conquerors through him who loved us. For I am convinced that neither death nor life, neither angels nor demons, neither the present nor the future, nor any powers, neither height nor depth, nor anything else in all creation, will be able to separate us from the love of God that is in Christ Jesus our Lord.

Bold Proclamation

Acts 16:4–40; 18:1–11 | *2 Corinthians 5:11–6:13*

Summary:

We partner with God in telling the world about the good news of salvation through Jesus.

Daily Reading:

1. Journey to Macedonia and Corinth *(Acts 16:4–40; 18:1–11)*
2. Apollos plants then Paul waters in Ephesus *(Acts 18:24–20:1)*
3. Paul's farewell *(Acts 20:16–38)*
4. Paul's arrest and trial *(Acts 21:27–36; 25:23–26:32)*
5. Introduction to the Letters *(Rom. 1:1–17; 1 Peter 1:1–2; 2 Peter 1:12–21; 1 John 1:1–4)*
6. Holy obedience *(1 John 1:5–2:6; 1 Peter 1:13–2:3; Rom. 6:15–23)*
7. Faith in action *(1 Peter 2:4–12; 1 John 3:16–18; Eph. 6:10–19; James 1:19–2:26; Gal. 5:13–26)*

Memorize: *2 Corinthians 5:17–18*

Therefore, if anyone is in Christ, the new creation has come: The old has gone, the new is here! All this is from God, who reconciled us to himself through Christ and gave us the ministry of reconciliation.

Building The Church

1 Corinthians 12:4–13:13 | Ephesians 4:1–32

Summary:

We all have a role in the body of believers as we strive together for love, unity, and maturity.

Daily Reading:

1. The body of Christ *(1 Cor. 12:4–13:13)*
2. Honor and love *(1 Peter 2:13–3:7; Rom. 12:1–13:14)*
3. Living for Jesus' glory *(1 Peter 3:8–4:11; Phil. 2:1–18; Col. 3:1–17)*
4. Endurance and joy in suffering *(1 Peter 4:12–19; Heb. 10:32–12:3)*
5. Roles of leadership in the church *(Eph. 4:1–16; 1 Tim. 3:1–15; Titus 1:4–9; 1 Peter 5:1–4)*
6. Warning against false teachers *(Gal. 1:6–12; 1 Tim. 1:3–11; Col. 2:6–3:4; 2 John 1:4–11)*
7. A few last words *(Rom. 16:17–27; Col. 4:2–18; 1 Peter 5:5–14)*

Memorize: *Ephesians 4:2–3*

Be completely humble and gentle; be patient, bearing with one another in love. Make every effort to keep the unity of the Spirit through the bond of peace.

Eternity in God's Presence

Revelation 1:1–20 | Revelation 21:1–27

Summary:

Jesus will return and those who do not belong to Him will be eternally condemned, but those who belong to Him will spend eternity in God's presence.

Daily Reading:

1. John's vision of Jesus *(Rev. 1:1–20)*
2. The throne room of heaven *(Rev. 4:1–5:14)*
3. The spiritual war *(Rev. 12:7–13:18; 2 Thess. 2:1–3:5)*
4. Signs of the end times *(Matt. 24:1–35)*
5. Be ready *(Matt. 24:36–25:30; 1 Thess. 4:13–5:11)*
6. Judgment of Satan and of the dead *(Rev. 20:1–15)*
7. Eternity in God's presence *(Rev. 21:1–22:21)*

Memorize: *Revelation 21:3–4*

And I heard a loud voice from the throne saying, "Look! God's dwelling place is now among the people, and he will dwell with them. They will be his people, and God himself will be with them and be their God. 'He will wipe every tear from their eyes. There will be no more death' or mourning or crying or pain, for the old order of things has passed away.

MIDWEEK ABIDING: PART TWO

You are welcome to continue to use this format as you personally abide each day through reviewing, reading, and memorizing Scripture. For Part 2, the reader is encouraged to choose their own daily portions for Bible reading or supplement with a robust devotional such as *Live Dead Joy*. Below is a description of what to include in the template provided.

Give Each Day a Title

Write out the Scripture references.

Summary:
In one or two sentences, summarize what you learned during your group abiding time.

Daily Reading:
Commit to daily Bible reading of your choice. A simple strategy is to begin with Genesis 1, Psalm 1, and Matthew 1 and continue with the subsequent chapters from the Old Testament, Biblical poetry, and New Testament every day onward. Another suggestion is to supplement with a robust devotional such as *Live Dead Joy*.

Memorize:
Select verses that will anchor you in God's truth and memorate (memorize + meditate) on them throughout the week.

WEEK 1

scripture reference

Summary:

Daily Reading:

1.

2.

3.

4.

5.

6.

7.

Memorize:

title

scripture reference

Summary:

Daily Reading:

1.

2.

3.

4.

5.

6.

7.

Memorize:

title

scripture reference

Summary:

Daily Reading:

1.

2.

3.

4.

5.

6.

7.

Memorize:

title

scripture reference

Summary:

Daily Reading:

1.

2.

3.

4.

5.

6.

7.

Memorize:

title

scripture reference

Summary:

Daily Reading:

1.

2.

3.

4.

5.

6.

7.

Memorize:

title

scripture reference

Summary:

Daily Reading:

1.

2.

3.

4.

5.

6.

7.

Memorize:

title

scripture reference

Summary:

Daily Reading:

1.

2.

3.

4.

5.

6.

7.

Memorize:

title

scripture reference

Summary:

Daily Reading:

1.

2.

3.

4.

5.

6.

7.

Memorize:

title

scripture reference

Summary:

Daily Reading:

1.

2.

3.

4.

5.

6.

7.

Memorize:

title

scripture reference

Summary:

Daily Reading:

1.

2.

3.

4.

5.

6.

7.

Memorize:

title

scripture reference

Summary:

Daily Reading:

1.

2.

3.

4.

5.

6.

7.

Memorize:

title

scripture reference

Summary:

Daily Reading:

1.

2.

3.

4.

5.

6.

7.

Memorize:

Also Available from

LIVE | DEAD

The Live Dead Journal ▶

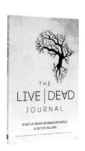

◀ Live Dead The Journey

Live Dead The Story ▶

◀ Live Dead Joy

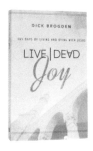

The Live Dead Journal:
Her Heart Speaks ▶

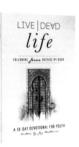

Live Dead Life ▶

◀ *Live Dead India:*
The Common Table

This Gospel ▶

◀ *Leading Muslims to Jesus*

Live Dead Together ▶

Check out the full line of Live Dead devotionals
in the Live Dead online store at *livedead.org*.